ZIRCONIA

....
....
....
....
....
....
....
....
....
....
....

BAD BAD

ZIRCONIA BAD BAD

CHELSEY MINNIS

FENCE BOOKS
HUDSON NEW YORK

Published in the United States by

Fence Books
110 Union Street
Second Floor
Hudson NY 12534
www.fenceportal.org

Fence Books are distributed by

Consortium Book Sales & Distribution
www.cbsd.com

Small Press Distribution
www.spd.org

and printed by

Versa
www.versapress.com

ISBN-13: 978-1-944380-11-3

FIRST EDITION
10 9 8 7 6 5 4 3 2

Zirconia was first published in 2001 by Fence Books.
Diamonds by Scott Dolan
Text design by Henry Israeli and Fence Books

Bad Bad was first published in 2007 by Fence Books.
Drawings and design by Leslie Minnis
Text design by Fence Books

Contents

Develop a mind that abides nowhere.
(Diamond Sutra)

1.

This book contains poems from the turn of the century. Written in the early days of Wi-Fi, when the billion consciousness of the human mind was first riding the open air, Chelsey Minnis's aphoristic, sly lines were among the first to crystallize just how the lyric impulse would come to really ride our times.

Even though the internet became a thing some years before it, 9/11 was the shattering that announced the present era, when something stupid, horrible, and intricately sexual would constantly be happening in some manner collectively, and whether or not you were paying one thing or another personal attention, as long as somebody was, then it, and its scandals, and the fallouts of its scandals, were affecting and palpably shifting the algorithms holding your reality together.

It was the end of L=A=N=G=U=A=G=E and the beginning of something else: something erotic, feminine, bored–pissed off, chill evil. We were awash in spam, the Disney-ification of Times Square, Abu Ghraib, and online shopping. We wanted to be the worst person in the world, but we couldn't manage it. (The police, Nazis, and enraged children have lately been managing it.) We were kind of aroused. We wanted to kill ourselves, but we also wanted to buy shoes, or become productive adults, and sometimes we aspired to innocence, to elder modes of personhood, but there was something antique, almost quaint about personhood, especially when this era of constant war was just sliding into view. We thought we might be able to slide out from under it, and also, we knew that we wouldn't be able to.

The effects of such a violently pornographic metastasis of all consciousness have not been, and perhaps cannot be charted. And yet:

lyric poetry remains a vital EKG. There is something about passing the world through your body and out again in lines and measure: a poem transacts a mysterious contract with the times. And when poems last, which Minnis's have, their capacity to signify accumulates and increases.

The winner has not been the one who most skillfully applies his intelligence and diagnostic insight to our predicament. The winner has again and again been the lord, in some form, of his own badness, and the architect of her own intricate self-objectification.

Her poems are full of honesty and lies. They are disarming: made of so much surface that the very notion of interior life seems quaint and idiotic--and yet they articulate a kind of sadness that we, with our personal brands, livestreamed mass murders, grabbed pussies, weird careers, social feelings, and sexual problems, can, you know, under-stand.

Her lines sparkle with the idiotic will to live in spite of everything.

Post-script

It has come to my attention that many of the best women poets in America seem to have gone to the Iowa Writers Workshop, and hated it.

That's what I thought rereading *Zirconia* and *Bad Bad* for the first time in nearly two decades.

These two works remind me of my other favorite women poets and remind me of the emails I get from women who write to me in the midst of their nervous breakdowns. There is a purity and vigor to their perception, which for all that fails to resolve into a being-loved, into a professional life that can be fully morally or logistically stomached, into an erotics that can be fully yielded to, because the desired object is a little bit of an asshole, or a little bit of a lie—the only problem is there doesn't seem to be anyone else around to desire but a wooden cowboy, a "mentor" with a belt buckle, or some other form of empty set, who is at once the addressee and the refuted/rejected nonentity that gives every line its bracing charge. I want you / Fuck you, Look at me / You can't see me.

In *Zirconia* the diamond bevels of the gaze have been turned inside out. The mind you're in is inside the crystal of ten thousand gazes, glittering. The poems are descriptions of arousal: they are bouncy, slippery, jocular, disdainful, luxurious, childlike and severe. Passivity and reverie: what does a cheesecake photograph think? How does a surrealist fuck painting feel? How does creaturely arousal remain lyric when its I has been smashed into billions of particles, fragments of consciousness unanchored by mere personality, but lurking like a strong vibe made of pieces of people, and can all this coalesce into a single speaking voice we could recognize as lyric while enjoying like candy? Yes. This is the style we came to know on social media. Chelsey Minnis invented it.

What was "stream of consciousness" compared to this? Said consciousness, once held within the body, has gotten up from its chair inside a merely lyric *I*. Minnis's I sounds like everybody else, which is why nobody sounds like her.

The exaggerated, real-yet-false feeling of simultaneous familiarity and freshness characterized by a state of aliveness that is "open to experience" but that is not, in particular, Chelsey (I'm guessing) insofar as what belongs to her as good belongs to me....

It is a beveled, shattered, mosaic experience of "what it feels like in the moment" and "what it would feel like" and "what it felt like," in short an experience of the present that feels Steinian in its smoothie of idiocy and perspicacity, which is what the ego really feels like, an idiot child, curious and desiring, briskly disgusted and peculiar, moving on to the next thing.

Bad Bad is a statement of poetic vocation, a diagnosis of everything wrong with the business of poetry, and line-for-line, is made of perfect, bracing, arousing, relaxed cruelty, like having melted sherbet poured over your head by a bored genius who knows you better than you know yourself.

It was an extremely important book when it was published and so it remains, possibly more millenarian than millennial, cutting into and through the spiritual materialism and narcissistic bullshit at the heart of all poets' hearts. Ordinary people, regular idiots, have the same problems as poets, which is that we believe we deserve other people's attention and think we can command it by basically doing nothing but talk fancy. We want to appear truthful. We want to BE truthful. We want to be loved. It will never be enough.

Ariana Reines

ZIRCONIA

TABLE OF CONTENTS

A SPEECH ABOUT THE MOON

I think, "The moon is mine and all the craters are mine."

Then I begin to think, "I am covered with drizzling grief.", "I have all the ice blue sinning birds.", "I control the sea.", and "Everything sticks out of the sea."

Then I plunge my hand into the air and say, "I want to eat the fighting swordfish in the sea who stick their swords in boats!" And, "I want to eat their swords."

Plus, "I like sultry avenging birds.", "Terrible birds with moisturized wings over the sea." and "I want to fight."

Then I think about the hazel waves of the ocean and the hot creamy lemon grasses of the moon.

I think, "I am going to sleep" and "I am dreaming about grey hair." and I lay very still for awhile. I think, "I can strew daisies in grey hair..."

Then I start to cry and the tears flow down to my teeth. I think, "Everyone has to bite silver mesh."

I constantly try to think, "Fish are resting in the sea." or "Some fish are just hanging in the sea."

And I lie very still and tell myself, "...In the middle of the night...it is totally quiet...no crabs are coming towards you..."

Then I sit up and cup my hands over my nose and shake my head slowly back and forth.

The world rises up on both sides of me. I think, "I have to die."

Then I lie in a position for a while.

The moon is flapping and curling around me.

I think clearly, "I have to lie facedown." or else "The moonlight is smoothed on my back like the map of someone who is trying to leave."

Then I reluctantly think, "Dominating bluebirds.", "...that fly...", "around" and "...melon raptors..." and "Tricolor murder hawks.", "...with their songs."

I lie on my side so that the tears from one eye slide into the other eye.

I say, "I have to invent warm tawny roses that have never been seen before..."

Then I fix the sheets which are twisted around my ankles and think, "I have to be tormented."

Then I continue to think things about the moon, like, "The moon is a silver hitching ball...shorn...off the trucks of the world...."

I tell myself, "...late at night...a placid sea monster...is rising out of the sea...with kelp on its head...to look at me..."

I think about the moon again. "The moon is a silver leg-iron.", "My entrails are the color of moonlight."

Then I think about the circulating birds.

I rub my hands on my stomach and think "oh no" and start to cry.

I pull the long tears out of my eyes and look away.

Slow blinks crash down.

Then I hold my wrist very tightly and watch the veins rise up so I become vascular in the moonlight.

I think, "Birds are automatically beautiful" and twist around.

I am dragging the satin around in my mind and thinking of my displeasure. I roll over.

I cry more tears that spread across my face and think, "No, no, no", "Fish are biting the ocean."

I think, "The thoughts are like terrible ballet teachers with canes."

BIG DOVES

....

....

....

....doves

are rolling out of my heart...and..

............just rolling out of my heart..

....

....

....

....and molten ice is twisting out of my

heart like a frozen.......drink..because

............doves are flapping...in my..............................

.......heart..

....

and hustling around...and streaming...long..............

banners of wrath..

....

....

....

....

because...

....what is terrible!..

................is diaphanous............................and whatever...

..........else I want to be.................................slaked..flashed......hauled..............turned

into a block of salt....................................placed in front of an.............elk and licked

into..different shapes...

....

...................or attacked...........and thrown into the.............sea............................

...............................and tousled...

....and flung.................

....so that the wrath spills out of my heart.............

in curls...

....

....

....and I am..

....lowered..................................

....onto.................

....sand.

....
....because............
I have come with the comfortable doves...
.................to accomplish..
.........my soft ideas..and..
....
...............the doves are shy..
....rollers......
....who roll around and feel very suede or matte and......
beige with diaphanous talons...
..............and are very succulent and available in the body...
.........because they flap around......................in the areas...
of the heart...
....
....that I want....
to be.............flexed..........thrashed.................................spiraled and....................
neurally lathed...
....
....
....
....doves...................................

come as I wish...

....

....to emit a pang..............of........

softness.........................and.......to load a.........................caress...............................

....into my heart....................................which is reinforced

by wrath.......................and soaked with growls...

....

....sashed with ache....................

....

..............and has...............................pearl...........inlays of doom........................

....that..............

.......warring...blended doves..

....

.........................must pull and pull out of the zones..

....

....

....

..............and then rove......around...

....with an overall..............effect

....

....

7

....of.....................liquid drumrolls..............

....

.......................and soft grappling hooks.......that pry........hard gasps off my mouth.....

.like shells..

....

....

....

...........................doves...

....

....

....with modern....opaque sides......................

...........hot round souls...

....and the ability to haul.................

...perfumed sedative material.....................out of my heart......................................

....

....

.............this is a moment..

....or an..

.........upward waterfall...

.....................appearing........and revealing to me now..

....

....curved............................

.........galaxy...

................roseate...

....

.........aplomb........hauteur.......epitome....................slams..........................

...................lasers.........................deep emotions................................

....

...............................awe...

....lucre..........................

....

....................napes...

....

....

....vales..

....

....

....

....

....

....

..........lava...

....

....

....

....

....

....

....

....

..........and anything else...

....

PITCHER

....

....

....................you have to take a metal pitcher with a wooden handle and just pour...........

.............the translucent contents over your head...

....and gasp....................................

....

....as the sting flashes sheer....................................

...........................and the water forms..............a square vinyl veil........................

.........or millimeter thin waterfall...

....over you......................................

....for a split second..

....

..............and the fringe drips...

........................like spangles or paillettes sewn singly on the edge............................

......and the pear phase..................of a drop........................repels.......................

....and then smears.................

....

....the bouncy.........moisture...........................

..........................against you...

..........and the fabric of your shirt is transformed by the drops pressed into the weave..........

......................to deliver clear panes of your shoulders and chest...............................

....

................and there are ringlets of water upon you..

....

......................as you fling........the pitcher down onto the brick road..........................

....and stand there......................................

.......with a cat intensity in your eyes..

....and wet strips of hair....................

....

......................and....................although..

....

....the metal pitcher clangs.....on the road.and.......rolls........

......................and.rolls...and.rolls..................

....to indicate the passage of time........................

..........the sensual moment keeps splashing and unbuckling upon you like a replay............

..............and the waters keep redescending........from an airlock...........to reveal..........

....

.................the spitting beauty of your face......

UH

..uh..........I want to wear hot pants...
....
....and rest my boot on the back
of a man's neck...
....
....and........
....take a sharp cane..........
......................and.................stick my heart...............................like...a piece of trash
...........in a park...
.................and...
....
....
rise out of arctic waters with curled icicles in my hair and a speargun..............................
....
....and.....................................
.........buy a lazy game cat with claws........................that scratch me.........................
....and......................................uh!.....................
....
....
....

....................someone should knock me down...and press me against blue tile...............

....and shuck....................

a gold sheath dress.....................off me...

....and push...........................

......a shiny buzzer...

..................to make me slide down a glistening chute...

....

....because.....................I am sique..............

....

....

....of everyone and opposed to everyone...................and just want

............................total emasculation..

....so I can...............................

....pluck the grey beards of old men..

....

...................................and...

....give them....

..........hairline fractures..

..............and a row of forest green stitches..................above their right eyes...............

....

......or then just...

.................bleed in a sailor suit.........................and salute them and faint..................

....

....so..they can bang

my mouth against a balcony railing..or...

....cut my head off...

....

....because I am too.........................petulant.............................

....

....

....

....and.......................................I........want them to..

....centre death blows between.........

....my shoulder blades...and..................then......

....gently lick electrodes.......and stick

them to my temples...

....

.....................because..

....

.............................I must..

....

....take a silken pull cord...............................

and pull......it..

..........................and fall through a trapdoor................................and...................

...............escape on a chrome war sleigh drawn by arctic huskies................and.............

....uh........................

.................................someone should...............................come towards me............

............frowning with a knife...

....

....and butterfly my flesh...

....

...............and..try to..

............................give me...

....oral...................maxillofacial kisses...............

....

............and then hit me with a brickbat...

....

............and shoot me........with round plump bullets................while I'm lounging.........

...............with a leopard pillow..

......................because.......................uh..

....

....otherwise....................................

.......tears slide out from under my cat-eye sunglasses.............

FUR

................I'm ready to plunge into furs..................and reject the standards of my past...

........which allowed no warm furs to enclose...

....me and no fur linings......................

....or strips of fur..............................

.....................................on bare skin...

....

....and I could not bury my face in anything soft

......................as I used to correlate a bad conscience with the...................................

....repetitive circular hand caress of

...a soothing material.....such as fur...............as I have seen it happen before...................

..........................when someone doesn't say anything for 7–9 seconds........................

....and you observe the cycles...............................

........of their hand through the fur..

.......................or they.............wrap a fur strap around their fists..................until....

......the sphere of musing bursts................and they say.........nothing to you...................

....which indicates a conscience ensconced.......

..........in a faux solace and limned...

..........with a relief...

....a conscience consumed with an undisclosed serious concern..

...............installed in a plush locus...

....cannot forgive itself........and..

.....surrounds itself with a valence of ermine...

....that insists on being stroked with sincere denial..............

....

...............I still believe in the need for honor and the refusal of fur stoles.....................

....but I forgive.........................

.........the desire for an inhuman softness...

....

....as many people are furious with themselves.......

while wearing clothes of the highest quality..

.....................and they are both disgraceful and touchable......................................

................................as they caress their sleeves..................and wrap themselves........

...............or embalm their bad conduct in belly fur......in the loveless fur void bereft........

....of anything except comfort..............

....

....

SHOCKWAVE

....struck by translucent lightning..............

....or........

.....................kneeling in milk near frayed wire..

....an icing white force................

..............bursts from your brow...

....splits and rustles.............

...................................and tumbles down your face.............................

.........................and pours over..

....your right eye................................

....and ripples down............................

....

....and...

..............shines like........broken light-blue eggs...................................

....

.......................and has.........................the very lightest glints............................

..........of scallions or pearls.............bouncing on marble floors........or........................

..........the silver lips of a feverish child.....................or a thousand feathers.................

....free-falling.......................

.......................in a room with no swans...

.............................or...
....
.............it flows like.............coconut milk or......a saline drip.......................................
....................down..
....................the beard of an old man.....who..............drank venom...................................
...from a vein..on your ankle...................
....because...........................
....a.......charmed snake.............twined
...........around you...
...........................or..
....you wore............
...................silver scissors around your neck in the rain..................................or........
..............were smashed with a vial of cream.............in the skull...............................
...........or a glass candy dish of semen.....

MAROON

....................my bloodsticky..................................wet..

....

....baby..

...........is...............an auburn...and............bloody......beauty...............................

............who...

.......shined......inside....................a slippery milky sac...

....on the grass...

...........and then...

.......kicked and kneed the sac until.................it thinned in a spot and split open.............

....and spilled out................................

.............my steamy..................................clenched......................................

......fine-boned...

....knock-kneed...

.....................................baby...

...............my shaky.............collapsible.................baby whose legs.........................

...........are creaky...

...................................and who is..

..........sleepy and strong...

..............with matted fur and saline..................................and stickiness...................

.........and is falling down...

.............................on the grass...

.............and is my cockeyed..............................lop-eared...................................

....dewy...............baby..............................

....

....and at sunset...............

...................................I am still trying to tear and bite and strip away.................

.....the membrane and marine blood as my..

...............................glistening rusty....................drunk baby blinks her eyes............

....

.............at the beautiful sultry carny show in the distance......

SECTIONAL

.......I sink into a reverie in leather...........................sectional couches........................

...........with caramel in my mouth..

....so that I am reliving...

....a moment and revolving........................

..............caramel as I am surrounded on all sides by.....................................

........................soft panels of genuine...

....

....................leather.....and I run my hand along the leather unknowingly.....................

....

..........as I oralize the caramel and soften it as I am..

....

....loosening and loosening................

....................into my dreaminess....with a far-off composure..............................and...

....

................................launching my molars..............into the cluster...........................

in order to.....locate...

...........the nucleus...

...........................of the caramel with my mouth and...........maul the unformed mass....

........................with my tongue..

..........and really lounge..

..............in the passive leather...

.....sectional...couch...with 12 separable sections..alone..

....

....

....as I try to evaluate...................the reverie...............

..............in the enormous moments...

on the couch made of soft skins...that are compressed..

....

....................................as I chew the mutable caramels....................................

....and clench.........

my jaw.......................................and demolish them..................................

.................in the durable moments...

....

....................with a soft formation in my mouth...........and the memories.................

....that are unavoidable..........................

....

............and the pliable anger......towards myself..

..........for lazing on tender leather...

...................................and hauling up the...........delicate past............................

....

....on the casual...........................

....

.......modular couch with padded armrests...

....where I can rest my arms

....as I revisit sorrowful.....and frightening moments...of happiness that must have occurred...

CHERRY

.................................I see you are kneeling..

....

......on the bone-marrow red.......wood floor...........and you want to grind your sorrows....

....into it...............

....

.........and twine your sorrows into the grain...

....or just cry on the bloodflecked............

......wine-soaked sunburned surfaces...

..........with the smashed and polished spirals of grain.....................and the knotholes.......

....

.........you are sprawled on the auburn woodgrain...............and the sunwarmed...............

...........dusty beaten wood floor...

....................with the scars of burns and the chairscrapes......................................

....

....you want to touch the warps and knots...

..........................of the beautiful hand-laid..

....thirsty...russet.....................wood..................

........and plunge into the whorl..

............................where the grain encloses a flaw or swerves...............................

.....around it...

....the beautiful burgundy wood..

..............fed on blood...

....with the long-boned grains..

..........and the scar of dragged spurs....................or the soft scuff marks from the..........

....drunk waltzes............................

..............the wood that resembles the swollen pond............enclosing..........................

......the thrown stone..............or the stain of the..

..................................expanding pool...of rosebrown headwound blood.................

.....that.............absorbs and throbs through the grain...

...................or the stain of the........punchbowl slosh...............or grown branch..........

....

........I see you are kneeling..............and raunchily........or ironically........scrubbing.........

........the floors with your.........naughty manual labor................................but............

.....you want to whisper your fears into the ear swirls of the wood.................................

SUPERVERMILION

............supervermilion...infrared...........
....warpath..
....
....bloodlines......
....
..............fireballs...
....
...........redwoods...
....
....
.......................heartshaped..
....
....
....
....
....
....
....
....burned....
....
....nothing
....

28

....

....

....

....

....

....

....

....

....

....

....

....

....

...............rosy flames flap out of vents..

.............................hot pink gills flare on the tropical fish...............................

....

....lathers.......roll up in your veins........and splash in your heart.....as....................you...

....inhale the....

....

....

....

....
....
....
....
........................supervermilion..
....
....
....transfusion.................
....
....
....
.....................lush...
.............uranium rays...
.................come out of your eyes..
....
....
....you wrap space.......................................
around your wrist..........................and pull it in..
........as.........wrath curves around you..........like a fume of smoke curves.....................
....around a cupid fountain spurting fire.................
....
....
....supervermilion.......................

....bursts..........................flecks......

....mesh..........

....

....

....rampage.......

.............................persimmon..

....

....{go right into **BABY VAMP**}

BABY VAMP

....brain fever...........................

....

....

....

....

....

....

....

....

....

....

...........all the thermometers.....split open and pour..

....

....

.............................they lift you...........so your head lolls...........................

....

....and..

............put you in the clawfoot tub with crushed...........ice.......................................

....

....................and....................................open the skylight.............................

.......so the fresh night is.......................................black...........and quick.............

....and the breezes shine................

.......................your cheeks..

....and a drop of moisture on the middle of your lower lip..................forms..................

....

................as you burn on clean sheets...

and dream of sealskin..

....and..................................

....burned mincemeat......................

....

....

.........you are in a dreamstate...

.......with...

...metallic sepia lipstick smeared on your mouth........bee wings stuck to your cheeks...........

.............and...............soft..........frizzed hair....................................

....

....

....

....as you lift your face up......with hot trust.................

...................and a fresh black velvet ribbon around your neck...................................

....your mouth like a sugarplum...........................

....

............with translucent honey-toned baby teeth.......

REPORT ON THE BABIES

A baby on 9/16 only wanted to lean over and chew the stroller bar. I have ridden before on the bus with many small infants, roundheads and chewers, but none so emphatic or singleminded with preference for the stroller bar.

I have seen four babies arranged perfectly equidistant around the table (9/29).

I emphasize that this was not the only incident of four babies arranged perfectly equidistant around a table in a public establishment or café. Also, more emphatically, I have begun to discern two babies on a diagonal.

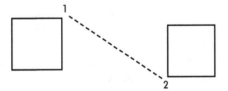

This is becoming more and more emphatic as the diagonals multiply and the connectors start to crisscross the city and leave marks like a grilled lamb chop. Also the obscene connectors are invisible and stick together.

Let me insist that I have also seen a baby with a red birthmark and perfectly calm, a baby crying directly behind in a movie theatre with no consolation 10/21, on a bus to Pittsburgh a baby could not stop arching its back 8/21, baby with pink headband constricting 9/13, a baby throwing down the chew-toy three times in my favorite café, baby who emphatically did not want the bottle, but agreed to eat a chip (on diagonal) 10/24, numerous babies inside baby seats on top of tables in cafés all over the city, one baby seat completely covered with a blanket suspected to contain a baby 11/1, also baby with bow scotch-taped to the head and baby with pacifier hanging on ear 10/29, 11/29. Let me more emphatically suggest that many of these babies and more are arranged perfectly equidistant and diagonal across the city.

Recently, this situation has become even worse. I've seen the babies fall in love with me when their parents have no idea. A baby on 9/9 was definitely in love with me and the parents did not know. A series of babies stronger and stranger than any before has been peeking at me. They continue to peek at a critical rate. Moreover, they seem to be enthralled in a rapture.

This heightened peeking has resulted in stress for both me and my acquaintances. One acquaintance recently revealed that she could no longer have lunch with me in a café because of the peeking.

The babies peek strongly when I'm waiting for my favorite bus drivers. They threaten to startle the bus drivers on their routes and confuse the dispatcher. The babies continue to insist strongly and you can see through their red hair they are in love. They say, "I love you... Come hold me over your head so I can swim... My parents don't know... I want you to have this chip..." Because of this emphatic peeking I almost went and held a baby over my head. They say, "My parents won't stop you... Swimming in the high seas..."

My former boss's baby continues to peek much more strongly than usual and says, "I'm over here... My head is round... I want to go up..."

I have tried to discourage the singular peeking but they continue to look at me with their eyes. When I try to walk right past them, they extend their arms and diagonals flow across the city....

UNCUT

...I desire to be pushed or shoved down....in a grassy area...

....and this is a real hope......................

....but it is not possible.............

....to be held in the uncut grasses....with confidence..........and patience..........................

...........as the soft patterns crush beneath you...

........and you struggle to...............understand your resistance...................................

....

....to the design of the grass engraved on.........

....the skin.....of your bare limbs as you are....................

....forced............to blend.................

.................the inhalation of the scent with the coercion...

...................into a prominant and unwanted imprint......................................which.

....

.......resurfaces....in the presence of the technical stimulus...................or else the nuance....

....

..............to reframe you in the scenic grasses where there will be no discussion.................

....

....as the...............

.......grass blades press into the underside...

....

.......as you are driven down with a knee between your legs..

.......and you are trusted and pushed down with hope..

....

and held...

....

....

....until you retain...........................

......an incredibly accurate neural concept of the occurrence..

.....................which you thoroughly misunderstand..in that moment ....

as..........the scent adheres............to your receptors....upon......................................

...................................the intake of breath...

....

.....................and instills the peripheral vision of viridescence...................................

....and an airborn internal knowledge.................

...............lands like a meteor and burns an outline...

...................of silence in the rustle...

....and you sink into......................................

...........a moment like a solarium...

....

..............and realize the honor...........of the offensive generous impulse.......................

..as you never believed you would be shoved against a soft green background to be admired...

....

...........and then instantly released.........from the...

....format of grasses.........................

....

..............to persist within the sunwarped dome.....of 2–35 seconds............................

...........until...

...................the timeline.........resumes..

...........the sonic gnats...........and the sizzling daylight..

....implants you with the conjoined dewy moments...........

....

............................so that you always remember the unfinished permanent interlude........

....

.................with the noisy grasses and the fractured octagons of................................

.........sunlight and the slow...............................absorption of the bee-buzz.................

....

....

....

......................................as your memory is now like a ball gown with grass stains.........

...because of the impression wrought by the insistence of a person who would not let you go..

THE SKULL RING

I am very excited about the skull ring. I didn't know anyone would think I wanted a silver skull ring. Now, when I am rude to those who oppose me, I can just look down at the skull ring. It has ruby chips in the eyes! Ruby chips like the nasty flame in my own eyes when I am insulted or reviled. No one will dare oppose me now in my hometown. For a very long time I have avoided rings because none of them seemed right for me. A skull ring is actually a good complement to my diabolical will. Thank you very much for the vivid skull ring.

PRIMROSE

...........when my mother..

.............................was raped...

....

......a harpsichord began to play...

....red candles melted.....and...................

...........spilled down the mantle...

....there was blood in the courtyard...

....................and blood on the birdbath...

....and blood drizzled....on brown flagstones...

...........................as a red fox bared its teeth...

......................white harts.............froze...

......and snow-hares fled..and left.......

....heartshaped footprints in the snow............................

....that melted...........

....

.......in the spring when I was born...

....

....

....

...............and it is torture......for my mother...........................that I am now luscious

....and she is dead.

....

....

.......and that I have...

.....................bare shoulders..

....and a flower behind my ear......................

....

....

.....as I beat gentleman rapists..

....

..............with bronze statuettes...

...........so that the blood...........................oozes down their handsome sideburns...........

.........................or slash them with a fire poker.............or give them......................

.....a poisoned mushroom...

....

....or corsages and corsages of gunshot

TIGER

.................spattered lilies.............with their...................recurved...........................

.............petals.........and suffusions...

....are breathless and....

.....dangerous...

....

..........................flowers..that you hold in your hands.............as you stride...............

.............through the garden..

....

....with your petulance..

........and your self-punishment...................and your extravagant disappointment...........

....

....

the hungriness..

of the bloomed............................flowers with the thrust of the florets........................

.....................................that are 4–6 inches across..

....

...............as you go toward them..

...............................you see their outward development......................................

.........as they are.................like sprung traps..

....the flecked lilies...........that you carry around...............

.................make you feel...........tasteless and overjoyed.......................................

....

........because they have no restraint...........as they are opened flowers...........................

...........with no reserves.......although...

....they get deeper and deeper in their funnels..........

....

....

....

....

....

...........and have the appearance............of a fine wine thrown.......................................

.......against a wall...

....they seem to be marvelous...........

........as I think about..........................how I want to replicate...............................

..........them or re-create their arcs...

.....................................or put them in a spotlight...

.................against a black backdrop..

....or lower them into.........

........a glass case........with a humidifier.........and a temperature control.......................

...............and watch the needles...

....graph their life force...............

....

....

....................................they are......preserved objects...

............in the controlled environments...

....under heat lamps......................

....

............nurtured and nurtured.....to turn into the desired unruly organisms....................

....you can place..................................

....in a beautiful.....unbroken vase......................

....

....or..............................

....in refrigerated trucks..

....

....as you like their.......................................

....expansiveness.............

..............and the difficult angles...

....

..............and the compression..

....

....

........as they express a generous hunger.........so that you may....................................

.......................not fear..

such a property within yourself or.......others...

....or.....................

...........................demonstrate an unusual loud vulnerability that is forgivable.................

........and vulgar............................and causes you to.....progress in your understanding....

..................of combinations of bad behaviors...

....

....

....

....

...............lilies with the yellow throats............and floppy leaves.............................

.....................that you have to leave alone..

....

....like show girls..

....

....the soft apricot/orange coloration with brownish spark-burns.

........of the daylilies.........that live in the day..

....

..................your emotion forms............................in response to their presence.........

...........and the fearsome hunger...

....resurged by the...........................

....oblanceolate..

...............unpleasantly scented...............................hairy blooms...........................

...............................whose bulbs...

..................................are...

..................dried................................in the sun..

..................and eaten with reindeer milk in some parts of Russia......................

STERNUM

........................I can perceive your bared sternum in the V...

....the perfumed...................................

....

....planar

.........bone with the...

...........jasmine hint.........has to be touched softly as I see the hardest...........................

....body parts as vulnerable...................................

....

....and the raw edged V is.............

.....splitting downward towards the reverse V of the crotch...

....as you.....................................

...............perhaps...

..............................want to be torn in half...

................rather than endure...the hurt.................

....of desire..........................

....

....or you want your plunging

necklines to display..

....how expectations.............................

....can split to reveal a warrior's breastplate...

....

....you cannot be afraid......to grab both sides..............

.....of the V....and rip them further to bare..........the revered sternum............................

....prized....

....and viewed in the rough frame...................

......although it is a simulated vulnerability...

....at least simulated vulnerability is bearable....

....for those..

...............................who cannot...

withstand unreasonable tenderness...

....

.............and I love the open V-necks of people in photographs......as they are unashamed...

....to be so beautiful...

.............with their bravery exemplified in the sternum.............as I want to press my hand

...................against it to reassure..

.........................myself of the bone strength..

....I value open-necked shirts or tunics.....

........because they launch the bare skin...

.....................and release the excruciating warmth from the chest...........................

....

....although you want to tear...............................

...................................the V down a further frontal seam............so that you.......

....can molt or reform yourself...........................

....

..........or just pull at yourself with an ecstasy like a heat...

....you want the tanned or untanned neck.....

.......adorned only..............with the carotid artery...

....

....because you admire...................

..................the drama of minimal exposure...

.........as though..

...............................the V was formed..

...........by an expansion...........of demureness...

....

....

....I prefer the unfinished edges of the V because.........the.....

..............frayed borders seem infinite...

....................and I cannot bear to refine the torn V.............or alter........................

....................the presentation of the exposed sternum...

....as one can only wear the unsewn moral.................

.......or immoral open-necked shirt with a beautiful result...

....

....and the deflection of the bony sternum....

.............like a display of a..........surface from.....which.......................................

....all the necklaces are torn off at last...

....

.........the naturally shining sternums..

...............................you want to wear..

..............a slit-front rough-hewn V...

...............because you desire the unconcealment...

...............................revealed by the flaring lapels..

....

....and you have the desire to widen the tear.....................

....

....................................and to deform your collars as you cannot exist.....................

........in common shirts anymore...

............and want...........the cut neck.......of a beaver-lined sack yanked over your head...

...............................and the bared void........of the..................................

............neckline sharpened...

.........to a downward.......point.........with the edges rolled back as you breathe..............

....beneath it...

....you want to be released from plain shirts at once

and shown to the world...

....

....with all the gold medallions removed....................

....so that the value remains with the body..........................

....

.......as you have wanted...

...............to trust your imperfections...

...................................and...............deepen the neck...

...............as you.....have many bare surfaces to unveil...

....

................................and yet conceal yourself.....in order to flaunt a reverse feeling..........

.....which is pride..

....

SUNBURNS

...............aha........the forgotten sunburns of my girlhood!...................................

....when I could not be touched..............

....

.....................when I had to lie...on clean sheets alone...

......and try to think...of what I had done wrong.............

....

.....................I remember when I was dangerously sunburned and I was glowing.............

....and everyone tried to...............

....smear creams...............................

..........................on my shoulder blades...

...............and I had to lie.....................................gingerly and gingerly................

....

....on clean hotel sheets......................................

....

..........and gleam..............with clear aloe gel..

....

.................as everyone else went to dinner...

....

....when I had.

...........................burned eyelids..a burned nape.....

......of my neck...

....

.......................an entire.................outline of a swimsuit.....burned......................

....

....and yet............

........the satisfaction of it...

....

...................the physical shininess...

....

....as a child..........

....I was..............................

...............red hot and very lonely.........

THE TORTURERS

When I was a young girl, my parents hated me and wouldn't give me the right kind of food. I used to steal Barbies™ and hide them in unique places all over the house, but I took no joy in it. One Sunday, my parents discovered the bridal Barbie™ I had hidden in the freezer when one of her shoes fell out of the ice dispenser into my father's drink. Immediately, they put me into the car and drove me away from the house, throwing the bridal Barbie™ out of the window of the car so that she bounced on the road and lost her veil.

They left me at a pawn shop with a carousel horse in the window. The pawn shop owner took care of me for many years and let me play with the antique spurs. I became an expert in pricing the boxes of cutlery brought in by disenchanted chefs from the nearby culinary school and presided over the display cases of penknives and nacre switchblades which I sold to delinquents. Often I would write tiny notes and tape them to the blades so that when the people got home and pushed the button they would see a message like, "The powerful force of this knife is now unleashed."

One time a vagrant came into the pawn shop and tried to pawn a harmonica. He said, "The music comes out of it like a knife." It took me a while to become proficient with the precious harmonica. I used to warm it under my arms as I slept by the various blue dumpsters on my way across the land with the vagrants. As my skill with the harmonica increased, the listening vagrants insisted that I play for them. So, every night I played and was not ever beaten or punched. At that time I wanted to swallow the harmonica, so vital was it to me. I became concerned with covering it with my hands so that none of the silver showed. One night I let the harmonica slip from my mouth at the end of the song like a jaw falling off a rotting pharaoh. I played until I hated it and that was music.

Next I found a job in a restaurant which sold daiquiris. My job was to slice the lemons and limes that garnished the bright daiquiris in balloon glasses. I had developed many callouses on my hands from playing the harmonica and so the lemons and limes did not sting. I grew to admire the limes and lemons. They were more beautiful to me than the burgundy car my boss the millionaire drove. One day this lonely millionaire came into the restaurant and demanded that I let him cut the lemons. That night I had a vision. Then I forgot about the vision. Later, I quit that job.

For a long time after this, I did not take any pleasure in life. As I could not find another job I liked and would not go back to the dumpsters, I used to stand on the docks. When a man invited me onto a boat, I agreed, but did not take much pleasure in the man although he was excellent at pulling up shiny tuna which gave me somber memories about my harmonica. My only interest during this time was to sit on the prow of the boat. I would often do this for about 5–6 hours. One morning I woke up from sleeping with the man who was not even snoring, looked in the mirror and suddenly punched myself in the eye.

After that, the man let me off on the dock so I could walk the highways. I walked the highways for years and passed several billboards until I came to a ballroom surrounded by dust swirls. This was the torturer's ballroom. I got a job as a mirror washer in the ballroom and washed all the mirrors with blue chemicals. As I spent my time looking in mirrors, I began to realize that I had never seen the torturers who danced and screamed at night. One night I ran down the slick halls and slid around the corner and ran into the small room that was the coat check room where I buried my face in the torturers fur coats. When the coat check girl returned for the coats, I hid myself in a long ermine cloak. So when the head torturer put me on I wrapped my arms around her like an ermine maiden. And that is how I became head torturer.

CHAMPAGNE

................you are alone with...

....

..........unstable champagne on your teeth...

....and you swallow flecks..........of it..............

....

....

....and then it keeps rumbling in your glass...........................

....the wet..............

................lukewarm fluid in your oral cavity...

....

....

....granular..............

....

................controllable champagne...

....poured downward....................................

....

....

....as you lick the corpuscles....................

..........or spores of burst carbonation...

....

....

....and rub..................

your nose with the sleeve...of your fuzzy.............................

....sweater........

....and push all the chairs...

......................out of your way...

....

.........................:.......and crush...

....thistles and thistles of soft foam.........with the fulcrum........

....

....of your jaw...

...........and swallow the ruptured....drink...

....

......as a translucent inset of your larynx...

.........reveals...

....

....

...........rivulets........in your throat...

....and you reach the doorframe...................

....

..........chewing the droplets..

.....................like the ephemeral gristle of triumph!...

...........as champagne trickles down your neck..

......as you are smiling...

....

...................the level ascends and ascends in more champagne glasses.......................

....

....

....as you are.....................................

....straining your cardigan...........sweater........

....

....with the heels of your pumps stuck to the balcony........

..........................popping pearl sweater buttons........

FLASH

you have to walk towards your goal...

....

....which is the opening split of a flashbulb.........

..........which feels.........like sunlight shucked from an oyster shell...............................

....

......and be..struck with the...

..................flashes that have milky fuses...

....and bask..

..............in the glare of..........silver lockets...........banged open on sea rocks...............

..........as the centres......................sizzle and deform...

..................and you replace..

....................................the faceted metal flash-shields...

....

...................................and the shimmering hammered...

....light inflates....................

........and falls upon you like a net..

....

..................................and the blackened cases...................................

...................crash to the floor...

.......after the clench of a slender fuse...........................a plume of smoke unfurls.............

.................and all the birds...

....

....fly out of the tall grass.......................

....

.......you have to face the tumescent bulbs...

...............as you walk through a doorway of shark jaws...

....

........................and flashes...

....hollow out the bases..................................

............of other flashes...

....and a thistle of light skates along an edge.............

and..

....................the light........squeezes and squeezes itself brighter...............................

....in a vise.......................

.....as............................the larvae of a vision matures..............................

.................and bursts the glass.......and blows.....................................

a visual glaze...

...............before...

...................you hear...

.........the croak of the flash...

....and you frown in your beautiful portrait

ELECTRONIQUE

I'm afraid my madness will manifest as paradise..
....
....and that I will have to be strapped down............................
..............because of my happiness...
....which is like.........
...icicles............................or an electronic spider lily...
....
....and I'm afraid my reality will melt..........
...................to form the liquid alloy.....of reality.....................................
......which is...........a neural flower pavilion...
....
....with..
....free-rolling Ferris wheels...
....
............................and an irreversible..
............pressure of temperamental......sweetness in the pineal gland...........which..........
....is like.......................
............a pearl-handled vise......................turned until.....................................
.it..

....ruptures...

...........to reopen the unreal palisade.....................or planetarium of lunacy..................

.......................or hanging garden....of sadness...

.............................where there are..

.........phosphorescent blue....butterflies...............and...

....black-eyed goldfish..................................

....

...........and a generated atmosphere..

.........that has......a vibrating.........botanical.............pheromone...............................

...............or chypre scent...

.....................with recorded.........turtledoves..

....

................or overlapping.....watersprings............................with the expanding.......

......hologram of watermists..

....

....as....................

............an alpha wave of euphoria..

....................or a moment like a...

.................................slit in an unseen bandwidth...

.........................or a flexed-open.....unknown seam bears..........................

....an epicentre.........................

....like a persimmon.........

....

..........as lovebirds.....unlock and cascade...

....out of the branches.....................

.............and flow and compress between the tree trunks..................................

....

....swiveling in a flexible unison.............................

....

..through computer-generated cloud formations..with pink/orange clouds..and lightning bolts.

...................and pterodactyls......in the daylight.....................................

....

....my madness remodeled.............................

.............on the plain muse of a white phalaenopsis.......................................

....

....as I am surrounded...

....................by phototropic organisms of insanity...................................

....or filmy man-o'-wars..

....and internal topiary...........projected externally.........

....

...............and electronically plotted..............clusters of tsetse flies..........................

....

...............I exist in a blister of fantasy..

.................and ripen with a dire....optimism..

....as the continuum of space-time........bulges.........................

...........to bear a deformed sphere...

...........................filled with the gloss of my madness..

....which is the illusion.......................................

.....................................of the lava flow or the supperating bliss.............................

...............of rainbows in a CAT scan..

.............or the implosion of a stained glass dome...

....

.............or the formation...

........................in my mind...

....of an atrocious....happiness...

......and mental gaudiness..

....and a permanent state..

...................of arousal in the blood cells............sired...

.............by the dagger plunge........of the.....fire-orange genital of the bird of paradise......

THE AQUAMARINE

The aquamarine becomes invisible when you place it into the sea. It seems like birds should have aquamarine beaks that they can dip into the sea and therefore surprise the fish. They could also sing aquamarine songs. If you borrowed someone's aquamarine, swallowed it, and jumped into the sea, then you would not become invisible. But your soul would become visible and all the fish would try to bite you. If you put an aquamarine onto any surface other than the sea, then it should be visible. If you put on an aquamarine choker and look in the mirror and don't see anything, then you must be the sea.

BAD BAD

CONTENTS

PREFACE 1

People say "nothing new" or "the death of the author" but, I am new and I am not dead.

Intellectual, anachronistic, superserious: I'm not going to start crying because "experimental" and I'm not going to start crying because "not experimental"...I just want to piss down my own leg...

And should everyone be bored like narcosis?....

Poetry should be "uh huh" like..."baby has to have it..."

If anyone thinks they need to write reviews, teach classes, edit magazines, or translate books in order to write good poetry...then maybe they should just take a rest from it...

If you try to write a good poem again and again for years and years and receive no awards, no money, no nothing...then you're happy...

And all these blurbs are for s—. Like if I were to carry around a turd and pretend it is my baby...

The poet I worship is Edward Dorn, because I adore his disgust...

Whatever he says feels like art...

Poetry is for crap since there's no money or fast cars in it...

But, in the thighs...I feel it...

PREFACE 2

You should not think of getting a job with your poetry...

If you do, then you will begin to count your own books...

Poetry careers are a bad business...

If you want to be hired then you will write the right poems for it...

I would like to write this for people...who don't know anything...

I don't want to hurt their pretty heads with poems!...

PREFACE 3

Don't mystify me with poems...

I can't feel a stifle for the rest of my life!...

If you are a poet then it should be foremost on your mind to say something and not to conceal it...

All this is for fighting...but you must like it too...

You should have something in poetry!...And you should take this as my first statement towards that...

I am trained to write poems much more meaningless than this.

PREFACE 4

I can only write poetry that is like a tuba covered with blood...

No asylums, crackhouses, jails, hitchhiker's cars, ditches, or body dumps for me!

If I find a piece of rope...I must use it to tie myself to the bedposts...

If I find the pretty pink horse-pills etc.

This is not a mini-gun with which to shoot myself.

You can say many nasty things about poetry if you like...

But Chelsey understands what is expected of her!

PREFACE 5

You should not fall love with your mentor, but you should try to punish him with your poems...

Then he won't dare to kiss you on the forehead...

Too bad mentors are like dogs but they aren't as smart as the dogs...

Often they are crying because of the truth...

I want to say in my poem that I am alive! But it is just a triumphant moment...

I loved my mentor...because of his ugliness...

But I wish for my poems to be understood as complete failures...if they have no loving-kindness...

PREFACE 6

Don't you think I realize the missing importance of this!

I would rather have a Gucci bag than a poem...

I wish to be a great poet...but I don't wish to be high-level...

I will never submit to the fellowship committees...

Because I do not like encouraging handwritten notes!

I will scold myself for many things in the future...but never for this.

I have dismissed all compliments since my mentor's death.

PREFACE 7

I want to write a poem because I don't feel very boring!

But I will feel like a stuffed leopard because of the praise.

No one should get paid to write poems and nobody should even be allowed to write them.

But a love poem will not fail.

Do you think I am very happy, with my uncut wrists?

PREFACE 8

I have a quality like that of a libertine...

Like I have a great desire to enjoy my own disgust...

If I am a poet I am the worst kind of poet...

Someone once thought that a poem should be more than an elaborate "fuck you," but I did not think it.

PREFACE 3

If poetry is dead...then good.

I know what will be fun! I'll buy your book and ask you to sign it and then throw it in the trash.

Of all the beautiful rip-offs this will be my favorite...

Poetry has to update or I will begin to rip my sleeves down...

Anyway, poor everyone who never went to Harvard...

PREFACE 10

It is very nice to be a poet...if you like it...

It is the frou-frou of death...

People say it is very dangerous to write poems but they only mean that it is dangerous to your career as a poet...

A poet is not to be praised for any thing...

If I write something then let me be killed...

If anyone wants good poems then they should tell me and I will write them...

If anyone wants to get bored they should go to a poetry reading but not mine...

I can tell you one thing like a 27-course dinner...

PREFACE 11

I am a poet because I have no other happiness than to write poems.

This is the tiny fake doorway of reality...

I like disapproval and so I am a poet. It is only seen in the worst dispositions...

I am a poet and so I should be able to say something true...

If you can ignore my vanity you will see that I say the only thing possible...

I am a poet but I would not ask anyone else in the world to say it is so...

That would be a crotchless happiness...

Many things can make you feel like a writer but not like a poet...

PREFACE 12

A poem can be too good for anyone. But this poem will not be too good for anyone...

It will be like a fake fire in a fake fireplace...

You might think you like poetry but you don't...

Again, I would rather have a Gucci bag than a poem...

I don't think my brains are that good...

It is a student's mistake...to like your own brains too much...or to think that you will ever feel bad for writing any thing...

A poem should not be flawless but should be able to bear the burden of its flaws...

You think this poem will have a high standard...but, like all poems, it will only be made to be approved...

PREFACE 13

When I write a poem it's like looking through a velvet knothole...

And it is like buttery sweetbreads spilled down the front of your dress...

It is like a gun held to the head of a poodle...

If I want to write any poems I will write them!

A poem that doesn't have any intellectual filler in it...

Like two blondes fighting on a roof...

PREFACE 14

I can say things that are not going to cheer anyone up...

Like, "most poets don't have any dick or balls under their skirts..."

But then I start to feel like a #1 jackass...

I can only write a poem if it has some punishment in it...

But...I have given too many unfulfilled promises of revenge...

PREFACE 15

Sometimes people want your grief to come out of you...

And you can give it to them...in poems...or they can count your drinks...

I like to work agreeably hard in the afternoon for plenty of questionable compliments...

I want to be a doggie of poetry!

My mentor was never really my mentor...

He was just an animatronic cowboy...

PREFACE 16

As a modern poet you are not supposed to be a spectacle of bad habits...

But sometimes you have to be hard-drinking...

Some people must commit suicide because they are too lovely to live...

But I am not too lovely to live...

I am good enough to be trained to be happy...

PREFACE 17

I can only survive if I am not made to be too discontented about my poems...

My mentor was honorable in poetry and that does not signify to many people but it signifies to me...

I do not wish to deny my own vanity, which is paramount...but I do wish to avoid "author" photographs...

I have a taste for poetic hurt because I tried it as a girl...

I was not good enough to forget it...

PREFACE 18

I cannot write poems to honor other poets...

I do not think of them at all...

If I feel a beauty that is like a swinging girder...

My mentor did not tell me to feel it...

And I do not like a lesser feeling...

PREFACE 19

I do not think anything is so hard in life until I am denied a treat or a gift...

And then I understand that my life is, in fact, unhappy and meaningless.

How can a person feel so meaningless and yet fail to disappear from the earth?

Every day this is a question.

If you have to ask something, ask why poetry does not exist...

PREFACE 20

I am a poet so I can say things...

And not so that I can have any notion of a literary lifestyle...

I don't like to be a poet but how else can I be so fitful?

When I say "I am a poet" I expect I am saying something that is neutral of all self-congratulations...

I am saying, "I have a special quality that is like swan shit on marble..."

PREFACE 21

I don't think I am supposed to be such a darling of death...

But if I love anything it is death too...

I don't want to make anyone's life hard! I only want to make my own life hard...

I will tell you what is poetry...

It is a remote electronic claw picking up a stuffed bunny rabbit...

PREFACE 22

You should never fall in love with your mentor just because of his belt buckle...

Then you know you will do any thing to appear true-hearted...

When I loved my mentor I was true-hearted...although it was totally hack...

He could only think I was playacting...

I did not write one good poem of love during that time...but neither did anyone...

PREFACE 23

If someone tells me I have to read so-and-so then I usually don't...

I don't want to criticize anyone in poetry! I don't want to break apart their rocking chairs etc..

I just want to be a sucker too..

PREFACE 24

I can't like this and no one can...

I want to be the worst person in the world but I'm not.

The thing is...I can't really learn how to write poetry...

There are many objections to this poem, but I hope there are no objections to the truth!

PREFACE 25

If anyone should write a love poem, I should, but only for fancy...

I do not wish for you to think there will be no bloody bunny rabbits or smashed éclairs in it...

I know you will like it like a piggie...

I know you will not become feeble with boredom...

A poem is like a retractable ceiling so all the shitty doves can fly out...

PREFACE 26

It is very romantic to be a poet...like having a bad back...

But it is also a pleasure... like squeezing your legs together...and buttoning your blouse all the way up...

But then it is too much pleasure, like peach pie

And it becomes...too average to live...

PREFACE 27

I would like to hurt the people who hurt me so well...

It is not a rosy sentiment!

I love things that are obvious pacifications...like drink...

This poem is so you can feel a true hurt that is like a gold medallion between your breasts...

I like to write poems...but I don't like to see through a tiny telescope all the way to hell...

PREFACE 28

Often I find myself defending my own narcissism...

But my talent is still inside me like an épée...

I only liked my mentor because of my own talent...

I wanted to kiss his hand but it is wrong to kiss someone's hand...

PREFACE 29

It is undisciplined to fall in love with your mentor...

It is like running away from a lawn party...

If you are too lucky, then you won't understand...

I loved my mentor because I could not please him...

That was a pretty lesson I taught him...

PREFACE 30

Once I became a poet I could not be taught to be a poet...

It is like wearing a slit slip under a slit skirt...

Now I am careless of my statements...

And it feels good...like a champagne bidet...

I should not have poetry as a vanity and I should not have it as a career...

But I should have it!...like a doorknob covered with honey...

PREFACE 31

I can't accept a reasonable alternative...I can only accept the bad original idea...which is to write poems...

It is very disheartening, like circus wages...
I want to write a poem like non-asphyxiation!

Sometimes I look inward with happiness and this is when I can write a poem...

PREFACE 32

I have been created to make a show out of everything...even my own disgraces...

Poetry is my horsie that I ride around...

It is like hitting someone on the head with a rubber chicken but then apologizing right away...

You can try to believe what I say in my poems, but your teachers will force you to admit it is not true...

PREFACE 33

I liked my mentor…

I would try to grab onto his sweaters but it was nothing…

It was like a sumptuous near-moment…

I want someone to kiss the inside of my wrist and then throw it down…

Because that is the hard detachment of a mentor…

PREFACE 34

Poetry is made to produce an expensive drowsiness…

With a true flickering of disinterest…

This is like a very serious boredom…

It is the boredom of poetry!

PREFACE 35

Poetry is hardly any thing...

But it feels good like pumped syrup...

You have to be a weakling to be a poet...

Like someone yelling and waving their lollipop around...

But...it is nice to drink at an outdoor table and watch your poems blow away...

PREFACE 36

"Poetry writing" is a hardship

Like crying because you don't like the wallpaper...

It is like bleeding from your anus in the snow...

But I don't like it...

PREFACE 37

This makes me sad...

But if I must have something...it should be sad...

I want to be gross with feeling!

It is suitable or unsuitable, I don't care

This is supposed to be a good poem placed very gently upon the desk...

PREFACE 38

I am not writing poetry to uphold a tradition...

People will give me a compliment when they don't know if I'm any good or not...

Do not ask me to be gracious when I am not trying to be so gracious...

I chose to be a poet...not to rise above it!

PREFACE 39

Sometimes I am bored by poetry and I am supposed to think it is my own fault...

But how can it be my fault when I am so trusting-hearted?

As a young poet I was well entertained by discouraging remarks...

Now I have to bark like a dog to forget that memory!

It is too easy to be a failure in poetry...

I have not challenged myself in failures...

PREFACE 40

I am lucky to be such a failure...in poetry...

Because...I only like what is manure...

It is easy to fall in love with your mentor because he is like a crippled tiger...

And then to feel an awful happiness like a broken bed...

If you fall in love with your mentor then you will try to punish him with your poems...

Which is a gall...

So you will be a very galling poetess...

And yet, you can turn away from poetry...

PREFACE 41

This is like the buckling knee of a two-headed fawn...

I know you are my favorite fool!

Because you are sentimental on deer...like anyone...

I do not think I can be a good person...

I have ignored all possible good deeds to write a poem...

PREFACE 42

A poem is like a clear vinyl raincoat over you...

And you can still be stabbed through the raincoat...

I don't owe anyone any brilliant poems...

But it is very fun, like spitting out caviar...

PREFACE 43

I am sorry to be such a good poet...but I will write a poem anyway...

It is like bleeding silently through a hole in a wetsuit...

No one should try to be a serious poet because they are really little earwigs...

It is hard to die without writing poems...

PREFACE 44

I have not yet decided to be happy

But I have decided to write poems...

I do not like to see a loveless thing

But I can write an unloving word...

If you promise not to cry like a little girl I will write you a poem...

PREFACE 45

I'm so smart like I deserve a kiss on the forehead...

Even though I'm hurting inside like a megalomaniac...

Even so, I'm not going to any more poetry school

PREFACE 46

It feels like there is a goodliness in suffering...

And that is why I go against so many things in life...

I have gone against many things in life...

And it has always been rewarding...

But none so much as when I have gone against my mentor!

PREFACE 47

Sometimes I feel such sudden flaming winces of knowledge that are totally imagined...

Or I'm constantly acting out how I feel rather than being a natural person...

It is like a showmanship to be alive!...

It is very outdated to be so drunk, but my poems will not be outdated...

PREFACE 48

Maybe someone has been staring too deeply into the toilet and crying...

Or maybe someone wants to pretend they have nothing to do with all that...

I want to say "uh huh!" and "yes, sir!" to everything anyone says!

I would like to say..."This poem was influenced by Marianne Moore!"

But, "I have nothing to say to Marianne Moore and she has nothing to say to me!"

PREFACE 49

I write a poem but it doesn't do anything...

It just liquefies my heart...

That is a fine thing like being horsewhipped...

It is my privilege to write poems during the day...

But I don't know who pays for it...

PREFACE 50

I chose to be a poet...

Because I like both pleasure and revulsion...

Also, arrogance, narcissism, ignorance, and beauty...

But I know one thing too well...

No one should write a poem that makes a person feel financially poor...

PREFACE 51

Here is a poem…and I like it like faux simplemindedness…

This is like a fishtank within a fishtank…

This is a booklette…

It feels like eating meat-eating flowers…

And it is the most disenchanting thing except for temperance…

PREFACE 53

I like things like bottles, rope, and cash…

Together, these things form a discredited happiness…

If I don't write this poem then I am the wrong girl…

This is supposed to be very objectionable but it is not too objectionable, like naughty beige…

And it is the foundation of all drunkenness…

PREFACE 54

This is a poem...

But I hope you will like it...

It is like a cougar locked in the bathroom...

I am only sentimental about my drinks...

And that is not the force of poetry...

The force of poetry is a freely said truth...

PREFACE 55

No one wants poems to be easygoing, but to be hard going...

And I can make it...hard going

Because I know something about death...

Death is good! But not good enough for me...

PREFACE 56

When I started writing poetry I thought I could be a little girl chained to a post...

I thought I could have a whole suitcase of pills!

Maybe I'm a dumb baby...

But I like to get away with it...

PREFACE 57

I fell in love with my mentor like a novice...

I was a nude girl on a fire truck ringing a bell...

I learned that lesson but I have not stopped yawning...

If there is one thing I cannot forgive it is advice...

PREFACE 58

I know my poems are vulgar…

But not as vulgar as gross pragmatism!

"Poetry writing" is a bad thing…

But it is not as bad as letting go of your drink…

PREFACE 59

I know a thirstiness…

That is why I go to all possible hotel bars…

Love cannot be put into its place or made to do anything…

A love poem doesn't have any praise in it…only love…

PREFACE 60

This poem is like a total lack of financial achievement...

You must want it...if you haven't had enough of it...

You must limp home with it in your arms!

That's why I write it...like charity...

PREFACE 61

I can never predict what will disinterest me...
But it is often poetry or something brilliant...

This is like losing your fur wrap on a pleasure cruise...
Or the sound of a music box coming from a grave...

Writing a poem is like having your own way for too long...

PREFACE 62

When you write a poem you don't try to say it is noble...

You say it is going to be a one-time thing...

This is the proper discouragement!...

Sometimes you know how it is but you don't like it...

Like a woman in a mink coat with a bandage on her face...

PREFACE 63

I can't live very well on big-time poetry...

This is a feeble way to go up against death!...

My last book was very bad! I wrote it just for showing off...

If someone wants to write a poem then I don't know if they should do it!

But I should do it...

PREFACE 64

I like to write poems and I like to get drunk...

But you can't do everything at once...

Poetry is appalling, like an eyewink...

I know poetry should not be self-indulgent but it should be indulgent to others...

PREFACE 65

My mentor was so good...he made me want to do a good deed...

And he made me want to write a poem...

I can write this poem over and over again but I can't write it like a fool...

I can write a poem about love but I can't write it like I don't know what it is...
I know very well...

I can fail to be loved but I can't fail to write this..

PREFACE 66

I don't like congratulations. And I have always dismissed other people's good wishes.

Poetry has to be good or I can't esteem it...

Like tight...unopened...nerines...

I am a poet so I can say the most terrible things, like ordure...

I say them as liberties for myself because I expect to be true to my self.

As a child I displayed a revolting servility...

PREFACE 67

Poetry is like picking your fox coat up off the floor and saying goodnight...

There are some very cut-rate lines in this...

And they all mean the same thing...

But I write it with a distaste for any other opportunity...

PREFACE 68

I want to cut the arms and legs off a mannequin because that is what it is like
to have to look at a poem I have written...

I think this is an acceptable feeling...but I do not always like an acceptable feeling...

It is like lickable mink...

And it is like a lion chasing you up the spiral staircase...

And all the drinks in the world are a prize for this...

DOUBLE BLACK TULIP

I have emotions and I also have death wishes...............................

....

....………...

....

I like most things because I know I am going to die...

....................…..……....   ....

....

....……

....…….......my love is like weak....black-legged lambs...............

....

....…….......................................

........I have never had the right to say things that are true and no one does..........

....

....

..................................death is the actual worst hope..

....

....

....

....

....

....I write this poem like a girl in a black wig... .. . .

....

....

........................but my heart is the heart of a true skunk.....................................

....

....

..........................this is bad fluffy thoughts.   .
.   .   .   .

....like the hurtfulness of chartreuse................

....carpet......................

........I must try not to feel a fake kindness......................

....

....

.....…...............................   ....

....

If everything can be explained in a note then I will write notes all my life and never kill myself.

....
....

....

I don't know if something good will happen or if I will have to bang my head
unceasingly with a stick.....

....

....

................this is the total conciliation of my self with my destined self..............

....

....or else a great phoniness...........

....

that is sung with a ukulele.....

....

....

....

....

I feel like I have been posing as a dead human being

....

.........…............. ....with my eyelids open......and my head at a doll-tilt.....

it is very sad to have to get up and walk home...............

....

....

....

the purpose of poetry is to seem as lifelike as possible so that you actually exist...
.
....

....although I only love nothingness.............................

....

....

....

....

.........I do not know what level of happiness I am on!.......................................

....
.but

....

...... my great-great-grandmother's name was Eugenia Hussy......
....
.
.
....

.

....
....think of your own red-bloodedness..............

....
...............because you are fucked...like ruby throated........

....

....

....like carrion you are dead...................
....and...
....all along you know it..............

....because it is....

.................................most foul.

....like....normal

....

....but.........with the satin on it

....

....

....like morphia...

....

....because now—50 years

....from now

...you're dead.............

.....and.................

....

it's so glazy....

...like you want it   to happen..................................

                              ....

                        ....

                  ....

              ....

              ....

              ....

                  ....

                        ....

                              ....

                  ......but then..................... ....

....like

....

....

................every day goes by.....

....

....

....

....

....

....so....fucked like a mazurka.......

....

and

....

....

....

so chastened...........................

                                                 like protrusive.............because

....the body is

....

....   velvetized.......by thoughts...............

....

...of the revolving vow......................................of being alive

.....................although

....

....

....

....

....

like benzedrine....you need to get up.......

....................and live...

                  in a sensory deprivation tank of subsistence...

                          ....so that.........

....you can be honorable   like graphic......

and sad like.priapic.......but fucked like contempt........................... ....

.......and..so sucked and licked like jelly....

.......with flesh like lubricious...................

like the richest

but the sorriest.....

.... .and so spurned like impetuous.....

...but it is totally foetid because it is true..............

....because, like modern, you're going to die.......

......which means..........no more surfaces...ever....

.....and.....no more..unfounded happiness...

because...

                                                                    like cirque......

you can't   say one more thing......................

          but go on with it......

like a malfeasance...

....
                    because.   death

                              plays forever..

.......so that we're..

.................fucked like lucifer......................................

....and..

........sad like alright..

....

....with life as a couloirs..........

          but

with a breathless effect ....

because.........

.......of the moments...........

.....   which are...............….......................................piteous............

....   but imperious...... because ...

    .mandatory...................................

....

....anyway it is malicious but effervescent...to live.. . . . .

...with the normal moments like..a waste.........

                              of overflowing joy...........................

                                      ....

....   because life is a stint.....

                                   ....and

everything...

              nadir...

                          .

                          there is   pressure to live..... ....

                                and look at how it hurts.... ....

because we are .....

.
.
so prefabricated.....

and

                                            we can't pretend to think about it.....

                                            when we know it like inseparable.....

....
                                                                    ....

                            life is a substance.......

and it is pure

...sacrosanct [in the pussy].........when it runs out

    .

                            .

TRUCK

..........if you are driving a haunted truck..

....

........with.........your head..........shoved in a sack of skies.......................................

....

....

....

....

....

....and the sunshine cracks...

....open like a coffin lid.....................................

....and...................

....flushes out your memory bank......

...................and banishes your face...

....

....from all the mirrors...........

....

....

....

....

....

..........if you.....drive an insatiable straight line..

..........and forget to wave goodbye...

....

....

....

....

....as the chrome...........

....

....flutters like a swan.......

....

....

....

....

....

....

....

....................................then you are...................... flickering. . . . .

.....................................with sunshine in your eye sockets.....................…...…..........

....

....................and floury chrome...

....

................…....................................and a...........................cracked open cowskull........

..................…...of skies........

....

....

..................................…...and luscious asphalt.........

....that feels soft......................

....

....

....

............as you burn very hot...

....

....in a dirty truck..

....

.................and forget ....distasteful occurrences very fast....…..........................

....

....

....

....

....

....

....

.........with the vivacious sunlight banging on the trim....

....

....…..

....

....

.........the truck is haunted because you're seduced when you drive.....................

....

....and that's why......

...........................you're riding it..

....

.....................................on tantalizing gravel...................................….......................

....

....a..…........

......truck...

....

.........that's.............driving by itself.........................down the.......................…......

.................…..lover's lanes.......

....

....

....

...............with irresistible rust......................................…....................................

....

.........................with a song on loud.............

....

it's graced to drive...

when the sun is alright

....

.........................on heartbeats of road seams...

....

...............with rickety flashes...

....

....and everything......memorized.........

......................to shine..

....

....

....

....

....

and a cracked open hatbox of skies...

....

.............…..or a cracked open oil tanker......

.............…...with skies in the oil.....……………....

....

....

...................with..a sparkling undercarriage...........

....

....

....and glove compartment stuffed with.....

....

........damselflies...

....

....

....

...........& striae of lightflashes..

.........& you can see the ghosts in the chrome..

....

...........when you drive by the graveyards..

....

ASPEN

..the past used to be in the past but now it is in the aspen grove

....

.....as a combined unit of terrific imperfect parts...

....

................................with the sound of whistling harpoons...................

........which is the sound of autumn..

....

....

..................and the exstasy of unconcern...

...........................in the........twig-cracking...…..........

..............day..

.....................................when the grove blares with the lunacy of coziness.......

....

...........................superimposed.....................…...

....

.................................upon a grooviness...

....

....

................treading...

....

....in a burnt-orange turtleneck.........

.....with delusional..........serenity ....

....

....and plaid pants.......…........

....

....

..........through the thorns of an eye-level sunset..

....

....

....as someone holds my hand......

....

....

....

....

....

....

....

....

....

...............in the split-level grove.............................…..

....as the waves.....

...............................of leaves crash upon the tree trunks...................................

....

....and a memory...................................

....

....

....…………...........knocks me into a plunge..........

....

....

....and a montage...............…...............

....……

...........................of flashing slides of a glade..................................…..........................

....and it is my dreadfulness......

.......that causes me to befoul...............................…....................a far-out moment.....

........with..

....

....

....

....

....

....

...........................bloodsmear

on the back of the head...........and part of the ear gone.................

....

....a glowy undoable moment..........

....

....

....

....like a ceiling mural.................................

....

.....................in the tenderly dangerous autumn.......................................

....

....with the raunch of sunlight.............................

....

....

and the leaves...

....

....

.................................so that....I want to get down.........................

........on the ground..................

DON'T DO IT SOME MORE

...I want to tell you a woe...…................................

.................................a nasty woe that is for sale!..................….............................

.................................and I want to be your nursemaid..too..but . . . .

.................................only for fun....

.   .   .   .

            poetry

....

....

         ....

....is a suck & fuck ......

....

...........................…...................…........   ....

....there is a smell of horseshit.... . . ..

and it is so so vulture...

....

136

....

..like you should jack it all off.... ....
.   .

                            ....like adjunct.

...and lick it up....   .   ..   .

....

....

for nothing like a stipend **$**

....and then

                                        grind into it like a snuff..........

and play it off................like genteel.......   ....

....

when it bores you like a recidivist...

....

this is a poem like any other service..

and ...

....

....
....
....

....

....   you know I am rigged for it.........

                         ....

               ....

                         ....
.....

.... I like to go stray.......

....

like a lyre..

              ....

                                   ....and..

.......no one has to feel any shame....

...
....because poets are boring and they play the chimes.............

                    ....

....

....

....

....so that I cringe............

............it is very meek to write a poem..

.....although it is a dupe............

it is a poem

.........................which is a trough....

where you can make your reputation...
as a stiff

.....................anyway, I am not trying to be human anymore...............................

....……
....
……………………………………

....

                                    ....

....................................I am trying to be smart....in the head....like a pissant.......

because I like it like junk......

which is only the truth.....

MAN-THING

....

....

....

man-thing   you are permissive.........

...........................and I

....like it...................

....

.................like nasturtium....

I like it like cavil...........

....

....

......I come back to you...

....
....

....

.. ..
....
.....
.....

but you get used to it.....

....

....
           .   ...
                                                                    ...

. .because you are a hi-low.....

                         ....
....
..................and ....I kNOW it...like disbelief.............

                                 ....
....
                                                                        ....

......

....

                                                                ....
....

.....   because you are prototype..............

...........and I'm very sorry

....
....
....

.........but I'm trained for it...........................

....

....

.

.

to want you like a souvenir......

.........…...and that's all I can use of it.........

....   you are to be

used like a sentiment

....

....

....

....

....

.

...and so retroactive for goodbye..............

although

it is like a bricked-up door to leave you......
....

....

....

.... only a thoughtless girl....
........could like it..........

....and.........then it is retracted   ....
....

.

because you are   a rue.......

....

... .

.   ...

...   .

                                                                    ...

....

....

.............................like a disuse.....

.................................and so like an aphasia..............

......and this is..sixty years ago.......

and this is ....

....a faux injustice ....…..

...................because it is a demi-madness ....

....
....

of lowliness ....like.....

.   ...seesaw rust

and anyway I do not defy it........................
....

....

....

.because I am free to be loosed...

....
.

....

....

....

....

....
...   .

                                                                  ....

....

.

....
.... you are . a man.......................

                    ....but you are a thing............

..   ..

                    ....
                              ..
....   I have become darkened...................at the tip

....of my wings

for you...............

but...

I have a new plan for you man-thing........

I have a new half-hate for you...................

I have a whim for you.............and it is a love too...

....

YOU LOOK GOOD
YOU FEEL GOOD
BUT YOU'RE BAD † BAD...

you're a swan............……...

....…...so carnelian...

....

to be with you..…....

....

...........................so vexing & vicious.......................................…..................

....

.................…...with quirts of leather.......

....and rock-roses...

....

..........................bad † bad like a scorch...

....

....it is curacao.....to be with you....

....

........and omnivore to be in love............…...

....

................with your crimson..............…...

....

..............................and your rogue...…...........

....…....

....it is blackjacks...........…..

....….......

...............................and being stabbed with a butcher knife..............................…......

....

it is showerhead to be with you..............................…......................................

....

....you are a terrible burden like a cello.....

†

...........bad † bad...…....................................

....it is†

....centaur to be with you

....

.............................and propane to remember it.......................…......................

....

....

†

.......like a man but like a dark schoolgirl..

....

....

....

it is quince to be with you...

....and...

....chinchilla to behave

....it is tiffany to behave.............................

....and

...........a transverse facial scar to be kissed..

....

....   †

.........with kohl on your man-eyes...........to blacken your tears.......................

....

....

....it is cormorant to ravish......

....

......you..

....

...................................…......................and a silent hairdo with a blackbird wing..........

....

....

✝

.....it is only to taunt you with your own beauty ....

....that I put a black dotted veil on your face..

....

....

.....I want to pretend you are a girl...............…..

because it will only last for a moment   …...

....

....if you will promise.......to be a young girl...

...........I will give you a mustache...

....

....…...……...and sunglasses...

....

....

.....................................but I will hold your hand...

....

....

....

†

....

....it is rapier to be with you...

....

....

...............................because it is crevasse to be with you....................……...with you

it is ravine...…….....

....

....

.......................…..it is nasty to wonder...

....

....

....

why you have..…..........

....

....

......eyelashes like a money-baby................................……..

....

..................................and real blood in your tequila sunrises.......

†

....

....bad † bad...

....

....

.........................it is chrysanthemum....too..

....

....

....

...................................and candy cane........too................................

....

....

†

....

....you're a pearl diver.......bad....

....

....

....rainbows...are....

....…...….........coming out of your biceps..............

....

........it is tight...to be with you....it is crucifix....................................…...............

.............…..................................it is a butterfly pavilion to submit to you.............

....

....

.............…..and a........

a star of hate in each eye..……

....

....

...................and that's why you have to be spanked.....

†

....

....

.................................so...

....fontanel...….

....to be with you.........

...................it is rhododendron...

....as you are a ruse....

†

....

......as you are B-A-D † B-A-D..

....………......you are nix.......

....

...............and tarnish..

....

....it is radon

....

....

to be with you it is chloroform...

....

....as you are a baby chick

....

....

...……...with your virile..

....

....and your icily..........…………….........

....

....

....

like glitz.................

....and...........

....

....

.....I refuse to believe you are not a schoolgirl...

.......................with reverse french-braids...................…....................................

....

....

....and.......................

...that I can't...

....hold out my hand to you.........

†

....

....

.................................……................so..magenta

....

to be with you...

....

....

....and.javelin.

...............to be alone..

....

....

.........................like a bad twin and a bad twin.........

†

................as you are a man..

....

....you should be............

held...

....there....where the eyelids close...

....

....

................anyway it is basilisk...

.....................…...it is............andirons and andirons.............

....

....

....

...........................……........................you're a shill..............................……….............

....

†

....

.......it is all like a dirty waltz............   ……...

....   ………........

....to be with you...............

....

....

......like a...deep pink bronze reverse...............…..

....

....

....

....like impish......

....

....

....………......and your...................

....

....†approval....in a tropical flavor............

....

....

.......but with slaps in the face..

like I promise you.........................

....

.........................you're a poodle.......................................…….......................

..............................you're a skunk...

....remember you're dark umber.............................

....

....

....

....it is smeary to be here...

...........................with moneybags.......in our hands.. ....running.. . .

†

....

.........…...it's all going to smack down........

....

.................................it's grinding me like days..

....

.... †

....

....

...like narcosis to be with you..

.................................with protons of happiness.........

....

....

like a bolt of satin rolled off a cliff..

....

....

..........or a..

....wonderland of black sideburns......................

....

....

....

....†.but with your beauty like a gorgon

....

....

....

†

I am cinquefoil for you..

....with your.......................................dark adonis....

....

....

....and racks and racks of silk neckties...

....to despoil.....................…..

....

....

...it is......

laudanum...

.............................……..with your nocturne.........

....

....

....because ferocious

†

....

....

....

......……...like crossbows to be with.you..

....

....like........

...the sparking rustle of a metal hem...

....

....

....it's.......gumdrop

....

....when you. . . unbutton my glove...

....

....

....

....

....

....

....

†

....

...................................…..if.you want to be so good...

....

....

.........with your cuff-links..

................and your minx..

....

....

....you're a chisel.......

..........like lonely..

....

....

..........................and if you reach into my pocket you will find a present........

†

....

....

....................bad † bad...…...............

†

....you must be atrocious

....to be so naive............like a fawn..

....

....

....

....in your wetsuit...............with black hair dripping...

....

....

....smoking a cigarette.......................

†

........with your loneliness like a marching band...

....

....

....

....with your.................................

......badness which is like a sand dune..

....

†

....

............you are...…..

....

....like a girl coming out of a cake at a party...

†

.............with your violet & vanity..…...................................

....

....

....that growls in my ear like a sideshow man...............

....

....

....

....

....

....

.................…......and.........................everyone wants you to wink at them.........

†

....it is...........undine

....to be with you...

.........like taiga..

....

....

....

....or a burn wound plunged in snow...........................

....

.........or a red velvet...

valance pulled down..

....

†

....

....because you are tricks.....

....

.................because you are a schoolgirl....I will take you to school..................…..

....

....because you are truffles.......

....it is true you are a shrike†

....

....

...............................like brandywine to grab you...

....

.......................and shove a blue plush...

....couch against the door..............................

†

....…………….................bad † bad.............

....

........you're a thicket..like squeeze......…….......

....

............in your shiny..

....like flash-flamed..........

....

....tiger-mauled tuxedo.......................

....

....

....

....

....but you are a hustler.........†

P-IRATE

....…..........the roaring.............blouse of the moment...........

....

....is chiffon...

......................with ruffles..

....and is a smocked chiffon..

....that you wear as the..............

...........................swans walk around you...in a circle.....................................…........

....

....and is simply a stylish pellucid object............................

..............which may be held in one hand out an open window...........................

....

....

........or look good draped over your frail lungs...

....with the ruffles at the....

................…...throat...it is permissible to breathe......

.....frosty..draughts in such a piece of clothing......…..

.............................so you can freeze with no regrets..

.........with the roaring gossamer.........mutton sleeves around your wrists............

.......that are fastened...

...........with precision...

....................a row of 10–12 buttons...........on the dorsal side of the forearm......

....filled with veins that glow...........

.......through the material................................…..................as you are made to be........

................a girlhood ghost...……

....

....

....

....

...........in the foaming chiffon with the...

....egotistic ruffles...........................…...................

....that cascade along a timeline to show...............

......the underside of destiny...……

....

....the irrefutable faint pink...........................

....................ruffle blouse with implications.....…...

....

.............................as the lashes of a horsewhip can be felt through chiffon...........

....

...................as the intense piracy is delicate..

....

....

....

..................you look around surlily in chiffon...

..........................because you want to show through more and more.................

....

............and the ruffle acts as.........simulated embellished bisection...................….....

.................to.....reveal turbulence.....beneath your...

...............unjustifiable good fortune..

....

....

....if you will be glaring.............................

....in a blouse that is floating.............................

....

....

....if you will say unbelievable things..........

..............…...............................in tyrannically fragile clothing........or.......

........throw breakable objects at the wall...................................….............................

..............in your membranous ruffles..

....

....................you will be aware......................of how...........................…......

..........................you could be struck by an arrow..

...........................through the tearable blouse...............................or how.........

....the blouse will sever.........

........from the mere graze of a sabre...................…..

....

....

...................................or catch......................on a branch.................

....and.

....................................flow freely on the trees.............................

Foxina

...........the women in the viewing boxes ....

as their hair drifts over their cheeks......................... ....

....

....and they gently bite

each other..

....

.... they fit into the foxfur with their pouts ....

....

...............................with their shiny legs.... .....and their springbok fur................

....

....

...........they won't get out of the boxes because they have their....ocelot fur........

......bare.....kneecaps and..

....magnetized hair..

....

....

.................and their..............chartreuse ostrich boots......

....and their.............

oblivion of chartreuse...…...............

....

.........................…………………......................as....they bite..their index fingers

with pleasure...

....and caress their weasel fur..............................…...

....

....

.....and stroke their pelts under control in their spaces.........

....

....

...................in their............strict confines with their...iolite rings.........................

...............…………….....................and their.........singleminded blisses..........

....

........and the.........   gold nameplates around their throats....

....as they barely know..............

...................the difference.between.aubergine

marabou boa............................and a................

....bare knee or...

.......the nubbed.......leather.strap.................................……...........

........between their fingers and thumb........

....

the surgeable lump   of pleasure like a chrysoprase.....

....

....

....true pleasure.snarling at you..

....through................dotted charmeuse

....

....

............no one denies them their hunks of citrine... .on their knuckles.............

their sloppy muscled bodies..rocking the marmot fur.rock.ing the skunk trench★

.r...ocking the buckle flashes........... .   .   . .…….

....

....

....rocking the...cheek tint.......

....

.................rock..ing the fur earflap hat..

....

.....................rocking the   ....……

....mink beret.............................

....….   ....

....……........rocking the........

....t.straps.........................……..........

.... .rocking the ballet...pumps.....................................

....

....rocking the side-laced.. .. ..

                                                                                .. ..

....with their onlooking sex fiends....…..........

......their.......emu feathers...

....the odontoglossums.........behind...

....their ears..

....

.................the women with their hinge joints........... ....

...........beneath their lambswool...

....and their...permeable chiffon   .....

....

...................the ginger tone..............of un.i.denti.fiable body limbs..............

....

...............……..............in their swimsuits............patterned with cabbage roses

....in their......

.....ball-gowns ★ imprinted with a.... single.... black.... pineapple... ....

....

....................…..rocking the rubberized satin.....

........rocking the ermine...   ....…

rocking the pearl snap.s..

....

....rocking...the diamond en.crusted................…................

....

....

..........................rocking the..white faille..............

................rocking the beribboned   ....

          ....

...........……..with their lidded eyes....…….............

....…..and their shining chins...............

....

....................................as they.......................…..

.......................fondle gold charms.........…...

....in their boxes......................

....................................with their...

........cabochons or their samples of lynx...…....

.................or their mouthfuls of fog......................................…….   ......

....

....with their ankle straps and stacked heels

....................with their   s-oft centered pleasure.........................…...................

....

★

rocking the......hyena fur..........

...........r-ocking the shir-red...…...

....

rocking the off.......the shoulder   ....

....…...........rocking the slitted——................................

....……

rocking the

old-timey

....rocking the nutria fur...........................rocking

...............the..

...........................tulip sleeves..

....in their boxes with their hip flexors..............

....

and their   prone limbs...and their........

.........pantfronts and their...

....

                              plumb leather satchels...

....

....

.........and their resistance   to being viewed.............in the...........

..........................…………chest-baring moire.....................................….......

....with their protruding bone structures........

....and their...........................…..........

....

                    ....   intakes of breath........................

.........and the...exhales like cameos

.......and their...

....

sacro-cranial vertebrae...........................

....r★cking the conch pearl

....

.............rocking the pin/stripe...
....rocking the

....fluted sleeves
....★...

............ro-ck-ing the puma fur...

....rocking

the crocodile-over-the-knee...

....

....

....

....

....in their boxes with their.......

. ...neck-bites................................ ....

....and their swaybacks...................

....as they...

.....revolve........lemur-fur...stoles..

..............and blow................oral . . mist on the box-side..............   ..

....

....

................with their.................... ....

....

....aerated ruffles................. ....

....

....and the numerous admirers........... ...

......of their brushed tresses......   ★

....

....

....

....

....and their.........

.........pleather   flares..

......in their boxes..with theirthumbs in their beltloops.........................★

....rocki,ng........

....

...............................the diaphanous...…..

.........................…..in their...........…..

.....peasant blouses......   with their...

...............…   ....chalcedony   ....…

....

....and their

oval decals of exhale..

…...and foxtails...............

and polecat ★   fur..

....

....

....rocking the jet-beaded.   .

....

....RoCkING the man-eating...

....rockinG the zebra boot

.................rOCKINg the.......................................

....orchidaceous............................

....rocking the chastE

...................rocking the smOking jacket................................ . . .   . . .

....

....   with their cOhering angora...........

................and their..

.................................straps../// ....

....and their..straps..///

....

.................rocking the naugahyde..........................

....

...............................….rocking the black pinafore....

............…..............…...................   ....

.....................rocking the mesh   inserts.......................................

            ....

.rocking the reading glASSes...…….........

....….........…..............rocking:..........studs,..........quilts,...............grommets,............

....

....

....

....

....rocking the pink, long-haired-goat coat

..................r,ocking the ballOOn sleeves

....

the women....................   ....

..................with their..

....airiness, gauziness, balminess, dewiness..................

....

....in grooved mink...

....

....biting....

....their thumb joints

....

....as their,....marled scarves,........

..................float through......... ......their arms....................................

....

...............their aureate chiffon like diesel fumes...

....

....

              and their dark.. ....

.......barely flared....nostrils...

....

....……...

....

..............................the...ovals of pauses...

....………................   .....

....……..   ..

................................in their mouths and..

....the............

                                                              morsels of sighs.................…….

                                              ...★...

....…….................rocking the thigh holster:.......

....rocking the lower..
          ..lashline...

....rocking the cutaway

....

...........................rocking the curtsey....

....

....

....

....rocking the pearl pumP,...

....rocking the tearstreaK....

....in their cretonne..

....

..............................with their steaminess...........and their.....................................

....

....rotator cuffs...★...............

....

....rocking the puff sleeves.......................

.........rocking the fur-pom-poms-on-the-toes-of-the-pumps...............................

.......................rocking the: fuzzY wool..

....…

....

....……..

....

....rocking the poinTelle ★

....

....

....

....

                                                        ★

                     ....………...

                ....

                ....………...

....rocking......the....

....

.............emerald...........mousseline........wreath dress.....................................

....

.......................★like undersea fauna

   .   .   .   .   .rockingtheknottedleather.   .   .   .   .

                            r.o.c.k.i.n.g........the bleeding flower.... . . . .

                            rocking/the grosgrain fringed.......…...........

....

...................……………..............................rocking the lilac raccoon........

....

.........rocking the curliQues of pheasanT feathers...............................

....

....rock-ing........

the leatheriZED-..

....double-faced-sable........................

....rocking the   ....the soufflé blouse

....

            rocking the hooks and eyes...........…...........Rock..................................

            ....Ing.........................

      ....tHe droP

....earrings.........

    rocking   the frock coat.......................................

..............in their..

.......lime empire dresses...★

....with their,....luminous exhale.......s

..............and their slithery lamé...

....

....…….........and their sea-anemone   corsages........

........................as they...want...............

....to be...............................viewed in their bodies

....

....

                                              with their mohair exhales.....

....and their...........

....…...

....spheres of beryl...............

....

.......................and the auras of shawls on their shoulders...........................

....

....

....rocking the crochet   .

         .   .   .   .

         .   .   .   .…..

...........with their..…..

...................shorn underarms...

....and their locks of hair.......

...............★rocking the bemused..

...........................in their............................…..

......................................goat shearling............…...

............with salient   aureoles....…...

....and collarbone shadows........

....holo

graphic with drowsiness..…

....churning in cashmere...

....

.....singeing their neurons with osprey feathers..

....★   ....…..........

....

....

....

rocking the baby...

llama...

..........rocking the ruby-buckled   mule...

....rocking the tighT cloche

....

....

....in their flowing suede..........

....maple boots..........

            ....…..

....

....................................……….................in the taupe neckwraps..……….............

.......with the biteable napes......................................…..

....

....and fleecy exhales

........and nuzzling gazes..

......which are like.....................airbrushes...

..................rocking the sheriff star ★...

....

....

....rocking the mechanical bull.............................

....

....rocking the tourmalines.............

....

...................................rocking the jaguarondi..........

....★𝓕𝓸𝔁𝓲𝓷𝓪★

MILDRED

Mildred, beautiful, like a harpoon

Mildred, my heart is hardened...

Mildred, the scalloped edge of your almond green leather

Mildred, with a stained shirtfront, Mildred, with a gag in the mouth

Mildred, drills are drilling all night long holes for your eye to look through

Mildred, the light green grommets

Mildred, the dragonfly barrette

Mildred, I am standing over your sadness at this moment

Mildred, the blood-rushes, the hematite and the turning black parasol

Mildred, to vomit in silver bowls

Mildred, underwater sunshine

Mildred, in a tropical-print pantsuit

Mildred, the geometric sadness and the keyhole dress

Mildred, mudslides and mudslides of solitude

Mildred, a lionfish...

Mildred, a bloody nose and a black frock

Mildred, ruinous and fresh as starfruit

Mildred with the plastic flowers in your hair

Mildred, your sleepiness like blinking lights, your sleepiness like cocoa butter...

Mildred, on unrepeating patterned carpets

Mildred, in bright yellow diamonds

Mildred, scarved and scarved with a flowered square

Mildred, on the sky blue floor crying

Mildred, piranha shiny...sinking into joy

Mildred, spiral sunbeams of blood in the ocean

Splitting your gown with the pulse of a thigh, Mildred,

Mildred, an eclipse in the background and your black lipstick Mildred

Mildred, the bristles of flashes from the back of silver brushes

Mildred, the burnt milk and the clacking of ladies' boots

Mildred, axles and axles of silence

Mildred, a black feather eyemask!

♥

Mildred, the retinal scan of an aloe green eye

Mildred, cabinets open to reveal you

Mildred, thrown upon the ceiling, a gold border surrounding you

Mildred, you can safely tear yourself apart...

Mildred, red ants in the grass

Mildred, the electronic verbena

Mildred, the night spurts over your black umbrellas

♥

Mildred, twisting to swirl the organza underwater

Mildred, pulling off the petals of a leather flower

Mildred, your eyes are green volcanoes

Mildred, the flattened grass, the backless slipper

Mildred, in a stained glass swimming pool

Mildred, unraveling: a shantung sash

Mildred, the pressure of an opaque, foam-soft madness...

Mildred, a skirt with the hemline burning upward

Mildred, filthy and grim little girls...

Mildred, the fin or swath of glaze in an eye-sphere

Mildred, algae and phosphorescent ball gowns...

Mildred, the funnel over your heart

Mildred, icy and dumb little girls

Mildred, the hornèd deer

Mildred, to float...with a buoyant hushed evil

Mildred, your thigh-high boots to stomp out the pestilence of loneliness!

Mildred, chartreuse swimming trunks on a gentleman

Mildred, limeade...

Mildred, a cutthroat happiness is possible

Mildred, the swirl over your face, the hair brushed back, sea-breezes of shock...

Mildred, dead soft...in a green dirndl

Mildred, there is a dazzling graciousness

Mildred, sunburned at the funeral...

Mildred, a summer of vomiting into the sea

Mildred, swimming in black-rimmed glasses

Mildred, the sumptuous grave

Mildred, the pulsating...mesmerizing...lustre of shock...

Mildred, fishtail...eggshell blue...

Mildred, underpants with ruffles around the legholes...

Mildred, the shining anvils of a demure disposition

Mildred, the pretty birds that dive-bomb...

Mildred, a black coat lined with green grasses

SMUT WISH

.......this is a low low smut wish.... and I'm glad...
....

....

....
....

....

....
....
....
....

...............to have it...

....

....

...........................but I am a coward for it...

....
....

....

....because it is too good like sapphire but this isn't the end
of it........

....

....until I get sick of it....

....

....

it's not too much........................

....

....

....
....
....

....

....

....

....
.... when you sit beside me... like ....

....

....

....

....
insultingly...

....
.
....
....
....

                    ....   good..
....

....

.... because you are such a   brunette..................

....

....

....

....

....

....

....

.............like
.... luckless...

....to be next to you.........................

....

....

....

....

....

....

....

....

....

instead of.... heavenly..............

....

....

.... with nothing.......................................

....to forget

......this is   .

....
....vice.

and ....

.

.   . everything like cassis   ....

....

....

....

and ....

....

.

.   .   .

.

....

....

....you know I am ruining it..

....

....

199

....with sequins
....

....

.............................which are like panics

....

and thinking

....

...........................what............

....
....I want...................   ....
....
                            ....
.....
....   like a torchiere.....
    .   .   ..
....
....

....

....

..........................is to have. ....

....

.........within the range...

.   ...   of the night.....................................

                  ....

....

                                        .

                  a caprice

....

....

                  .

like peril.....

....................with you..

....because you are ....

                                                        ....
....
....a reek................

                                        ....

....

                                                                ....

                  ....and I'm

... stupefied......................... .because.........

....

....

....

....

.... you ..are next to me

. . . like meteoric.............................for a while..............

....

....

....

....

. ...because.

.. ..

....

....

....

....

like dishonor! you look good...

....

....

....

....

at night

....

when you are not for me...

....

....

....

....

....

....

....

....

....

.....

....and

...............this is like a smash-up.............

....   when I want to have you
but I

.... disavow it...

because you are a.pearl...........and I

like you like sideways.........

....

....

....

....

                                                    ....
                                            ....

...   .

....

.... but so much that I wish..
    .
    .
    .
    .

                like fallible................   ....

,..............to

....

       have you like punish...

....

....

       ....

       ....

       ....

....

       ....

....

because.

.......I have ....a

... .smut...........wish.......... for you................ like dismay.........

....
.........and I like you like...exterior...

....

F-LUTE

I am the most merciless girl flautist in the orchestra…

I am neutral of love and neutral of death…

The flute slides through my hands and clicks into place…

I have my eyes on you….but my lips are only for the flute…

MEN CRY BECAUSE OF THE HEAT

As soon as they wake up...they barely lift their heads...and then just start crying...

At first you think it is an enchanted misery...but it is the heat...

They have to sit on the side of the bed...and clamp their hands onto their faces...
and then pry their hands off...their faces...and look at you...

Chunks of tears...slide down their cheeks...at a slow speed...

When you show them a curling iron they start crying...and when you try to
brush their hair they start crying...but when they see a piece of ice...they become
completely still and flared...

...and they try to shake their fists...

If a bird lands on their shoulder...they don't even think about it...they can't realize
anything...about birds...

If you try to give them a kiss...it just sizzles on their cheek...

When you fight...with them...in the evening...they just agree with you...and agree
with you more and more...and sink down...

They look at all their muscles and start crying...

You have to cut their shirts into half-shirts...

CLOWN

It seems that I'm growing more and more like a clown. First of all, I'm always sad. Secondly, all my knives are made out of rubber. Thirdly, it's like my house is on fire.

No, I'm definitely becoming more like a clown. I have a tendency to want to put on clown clothes. As soon as I put the clown clothes on I feel faintly happier...

Another sign is that I constantly feel like I'm alone in a dressing room. Most of the time I feel amused. Anyway, the only thing good about the circus is the tigers.

I realize that I could get both legs cut off by the circus train or get frightened by an elephant. But it's very depressing to sit around in a clown suit and think about death.

Sometimes I don't feel happy unless I'm in my clown suit. And I enjoy hitting people on the head with a foam club. I really do...

When people see me they realize that it looks very sophisticated to wear a clown suit and smoke a cigarette. This is how I get all the ladies because they think I'm very droll.

People don't understand how you turn into a clown. You turn into a clown because you feel more and more like putting on a clown suit. When you're around people you sense a kindliness. It makes you so nervous you can't stay calm. Which is why it feels perfectly normal to wear orange pants.

Plus, it's very subversive to wear bow ties. You can't imagine how jolly everything is. And the fright wigs... I don't want to be a clown but I'm sure to be one. My mother was a clown.

FIFI, NO, NO

"Fifi, I thought I told you to stop touching me with your soft little hands..."

Fifi: "The weakness of Fifi..."

"Fifi, it is not possible for you to continue behaving in this manner..."

I am fallen in love with by a young girl: Fifi.

	Fifi		
takes hand	strokes hair	sits too close	puts hand on knee

1. Fifi should not touch my breast with her hand...

It is very very depressing when Fifi falls on her face on the flagstones and doesn't cry.

We don't like to hold each other's hands and dance with sparklers!

"She is a girl but she is Fifi."

Fifi again
        — touching with hands
        — holding face still to try to kiss it
        — whispering
        — petting hair with delight

Fifi, go away with your sparklers, I am not for you...

"Fifi at night!... Fifi at night!..."

Fifi: eating a hamburger...

Fifi, infidel of nothing

Fifi of the iron will of caressing

No acceptance of refusals, no allowances, no resistance, no taking away of the hand, no.

All this foretelling a bad end: Fifi to be completely patronized and tolerated by everybody, which is a disgrace...

P. CHELSEY

P. Chelsey doesn't like parties. Her state of mind is usually bad. She tries to eat hors d'oeuvres. Of course she wants to get drunk and berate everyone. But P. Chelsey has ahold of herself and things are going to be O.K.

If P. Chelsey likes anyone she follows them around and stands right behind them. When she pretends to talk to people, she is really just taking more and more sips of wine. If P. Chelsey doesn't like someone, she can never forgive them. P. Chelsey hates people for turning their back to her right after saying something nice. She also hates them for staring at her too long with haunted looks in their eye. Sometimes people give her too many compliments at the beginning of the night. Then there is nothing to say for the rest of the night.

P. Chelsey hates people who look at her pityingly and have bad breath. People wonder where her psychiatrist is. P. Chelsey tries to be patient with her psychiatrist, but a psychiatrist cannot be reasoned with. As it stands the psychiatrist is usually not at his office.

FRIENDSHIP

When I am alone...I eat all white foods...and sing the numbers to myself... and sing all the letters to myself...and count my own fingers....

I am waiting all night for you to come out the side door...

We should become very good friends and never say a dirty thing to each other...

You can sit on your swivel stool and I can sit on my swivel stool.

This is because we are wearing our sweater-vests. And we smell good.

We will be great friends and we will look in the window of the playhouse and see ourselves together...

I think we should walk in the rain under a giant umbrella.

We can share a microscope.

And we don't have to do anything but play the piano with a metronome and turn the page.

It makes us gently say goodnight.

And all of this is wrapped up in butcher paper.

I have no thought of cleaning up a mess in your lap. Or of letting my curls fall forward ever...

And you can never pretend to read a blank page...

We toast each other with teacups because we are successes...

This is not like a bloody shoehorn...

We are very calm and so the milk truck delivers all the milk...

We are friends and it turns us quite pale...

We are friends and we eat ice creams together...

It is always very calm when we sit side by side on the piano bench...

I want to squeeze my hands together but there's nothing to do...

Everything is an object that can be picked up and put down again.

We don't want to mess up our outfits. And we like to play checkers.

We are two friends who hold hands in the universe...

C-PASSION

I notice too many people recommend me to compassion so that I am accustomed to considering myself ruthless...

I sincerely believe there is no reprieve from the summons for compassion as one is supposed to improve...

I'm weary with the idea of compassion as a salve to my critical nature...which is my only refuge from the delusions of virtue...

The expression of compassion lends propriety and elegance to the expressor...as its distribution stems from a natural assumption of privilege...and there is a pernicious extravagance of compassion in sedate personalities...

Someone tries to instruct you...as you are supposed to be capable of it...and you blink your lovely yellow eyes...

Compassion is an expectation...even though one's temperament may be ill-suited to suave virtues...and one's experiences...don't form one to become the presenter of swanlike compassion...

Compassion is devoid of any thermal relief...and destroys the best defensive countermeasures...and calls upon one to rationalize the mediocrity of one's tormentors...

Some imagine they will find the experience charming...and prefer not to be grieved by endless furies on unchangeable topics...

I have no compassion for anyone who advocates it...as they don't consider the requirements of sincerity...and because such people are irresponsible with other people's mental health...

I could easily crush a moon rock in my hand with an...intensity which is alarming...

I dread lessons in compassion as they promote laziness...as compassion bastes the facts with a shimmer...as one cannot admit the dominant offenses committed against them...which account for their touchiness...

Compassion is a boast...of insight and serenity which is unfair...

I am currently not agreeable to it...but offer my revenge like a tray of cigars...

13

You are dead on the red shag carpet and the fish tank is shattered...

You can feel fine now because you are finally dead. And that is good enough for you & you don't even care about the fish...

One of your shoes fell off and your expression became very annoyed after you were dead.

But you don't have to look good now.... And you don't have to be in love...

You don't have to feel like a ridiculous person constantly made fun of by a parrot..

All you have to do is continue being dead ...

You're not so lucky but you don't need to be lucky ever again...

16

If you do not fall in love everyone will think you are too romantic to fall in love..

But, I don't see how you are supposed to finish your sentences...

It feels like a serving spoon is stuck in your heart...

There needs to be something inside you so that you are more than a dressmaker's dummy.

Something...like a bright wall and the sky darkening behind it...

If you don't dismiss your vanity, you will never become a serious woman...

The future can't be hated, and that is why you are growing old...

I know you are smart, and you are even smart enough for death...

33

Just as the other poets cause you disgust...so too do you cause them a disgust...

You lack the basic ability to live...it seems petty and stupid...to you...

But haven't you turned away from every fellow man?

What do you think can be a finite happiness? If someone knocks you on the head then that can be a finite happiness...

Do not wish for anyone to be greater than yourself...content yourself with your own greatness...

You will not find yourself under-valued or over-valued by god...

Do not think you will have any humility left after you have written your poems...

Do not attempt to be pretty...death will be pretty enough for you...

69

Which is more important, your fancies or nature?...

If you try to think you will find yourself overworked...

For this you will be hurt and all your praises will be taken away from you...

Someone wearing a bikini under a fur coat is more meaningful than you are...

But you should just keep quiet, otherwise you will make everyone feel quite stupid...

You can be slapped on the cheek, pinched, and have your arm twisted behind your back, but you can still say exactly what you want no matter how unwelcome...

It will be a great accomplishment if you will agree never to be married...

It seems that you are about to hang or shoot yourself. But do not hang or shoot yourself and keep on living...

DUNG CART

I like poetry but it is a dung cart. I like being in love but that is a dung cart too. I have to be content with things that are dung carts although I really want something that is not a dung cart. Something that will allow me to live when my frivolousness is like death...

Unfortunately for me, everything is going to be called a dung cart. Such as: kissing someone and then not listening to what they're saying. I don't care what they're saying! They're a businessman! A businessman is not a dung cart...

I am always thinking of a dung cart. Dung is neatly piled on it! Even if I look around I can still see clearly that everything is a dung cart & I too am a dung cart.

Dung cart after dung cart rolling by......

Anyway, I like dung carts. My favorite things are dung carts. Dung carts with dung falling off them.

ANTI VITAE

1977–1984

Nothing of interest.

1984

Performed poorly in math. Taken aside by math teacher. Receded into mediocrity of math.

D+ in conduct.

1985–1988

College application rejected by Cornell, Tufts, Northwestern University, Dartmouth etc...

45% in math.

1989

Fail to appear for graduate creative writing workshop. Class discusses poem without me.

Mispronounce "Kant."

1990

Unimpressive academic performance. Idle.

Lose essay contest.

Fail to get any recommendations from professors for graduate school. All applications rejected.

1991–1992

Mental health questioned.

1993

Accidentally knock over bookcase.
Called "The Most Abrasive Person Ever Met."

Fail to win prize.

Told poems "lack agency." Have to ask what "agency"
means. Don't know what "trope"means. Mispronounce
"geodesic."

Poems are called "Disneyesque."

1994

"Insidious."

"Ferrari without steering wheel."

Lose poetry contest under pseudonym.

1995

Poems rejected by *Paris Review, Poetry Magazine, The New
Yorker, New American Writing, Fine Madness, Black Warrior
Review,* etc.

Sit outside local bar and flash cigarette lighter at firefly.

Intensely disliked by older female fiction writer.

Told that poetry is "loose" by future poet laureate.

Commitment to waitressing questioned.

1994–1995

Receive no answer from "City Lights" manuscript query.

1995

Receive shocked response at poor physical appearance.

Lose National Poetry Series, Walt Whitman Award, Yale Younger poets series, Pittsburgh prize, etc.

1996

No car.

Apply for no teaching jobs. Don't publish book.

1997–2000

Continue to not publish book.

Bite cuticles.

Manuscript rejected by Verse Press.

Mental health questioned.

2001

Don't receive NEA grant.

Fail to send any new work to literary magazines. Not published in any magazines.

2002–2003

No teaching experience.

2004

2nd book still not published...

SAD-0

My sadness feels like heavy earrings that makes my head ache.

Someday I would like to spend too much money on a shag rug so that I could lie down upon it and not smell one scent from my childhood.

When I'm about to get angry, that's when I start to feel good...

I stare out the window, unprincipled as a tiger...

If anyone tries to comfort me I will vomit on the balustrade.

If anyone asks me why I'm like this I will say "im gon tu kil u!!!"

As a child I totally squandered my love on my parents and was, as a result, crucified on a cross†.

I will spit out my food if anyone tries to imply anything...

Sometimes an arrow starts to come out of my head like I'm bored → I'm bored → And then another arrow comes out like I want to read a book ↑ I want to read a book ↑

I try to stay bored for a while but then I start to become amused...

I want to put makeup on people's eyes so they can look like damned darlings...

People keep talking...But it is hard to stop them when I only want to be petted...

I can barely listen to what they're talking about. They're talking about someone who wants them...

YOU RAISED ME UP

Ha! You raised me up.......

and now I'm overflowing with good..........................

You made some food

and got in there

and said some things...

to a child

but alright you raised me up.......................

You bought some clothes

and took me around

and put me to work....

You want me to say you raised me up?

I'm raised up, arent' I?

Here I am,

raised all the way up

by you, as you say it.

And overflowing with good.............................

Only it's true I got raised by time

time raised me and I'm time's baby girl

Or you raised me up

and taught me how to feed the chickens

but that is just a farmhouse fantasy.................

But alright then you raised me

and I'm up here now

I'm not even biting my knuckles..

Hey you raised me

straight up and did

some things

but

that's all over now..

I'm up from being a delicate child

everyone's getting raised up

whether they want to or not

or whether they're any good for it..........................

Did I ever say thank you

for raising me up so that

I can say my own name?

But that's alright...

I'm not crying anymore

& you can't

raise me again...

-5 (NEGATIVE 5)

−5 for debating
−5 for misuse of the tractor
−5 for altering the chore list
−5 for pinecone throwing
−5 for misplacing shoes and other personal property...
−5 for delaying, kicking dirt, separating, tossing thermos off lookout rest-point,
   non-listening...
−5 for cracking twigs
−5 for excessive yawning
−5 for loud whistling, touching people's hats without permission, putting Jared's
   comb into the fire, misuse of the grill tongs, burning, failing to comply with
   cleanliness of common area, spilling trash...
−5 for improper conduct while fishing...
−5 for euphoria, obstruction of doorways, fire hazard...
−5 for "misplacing" trail map
−5 for scattering birds, meaningless interjections during staff meeting, lingering
   and/or petting the guide dogs...
−5 for delayed objections
−5 for exaggerated enthusiasm about trail walk
−5 for tracking mud, solitariness, obsession with fishing lures, reluctance,
   inability to initiate social interaction, furtiveness, secrecy, paleness...
−5 for loud humming during rest hour, loud buzzing or humming sound,
   destructive theorizing, misuse of and/or staring out of windows...
−5 for refusal to read information packets, emotional recklessness, bad
   sportsmanship, lateness...
−5 for improper storage of personal food, repudiation, defacement, refusal to
   return group mascot, lack of effort at horseshoes, hoarding the first aid kit,
   contradictions, negligence, spitting...
−5 for misuse of the fly swatter...

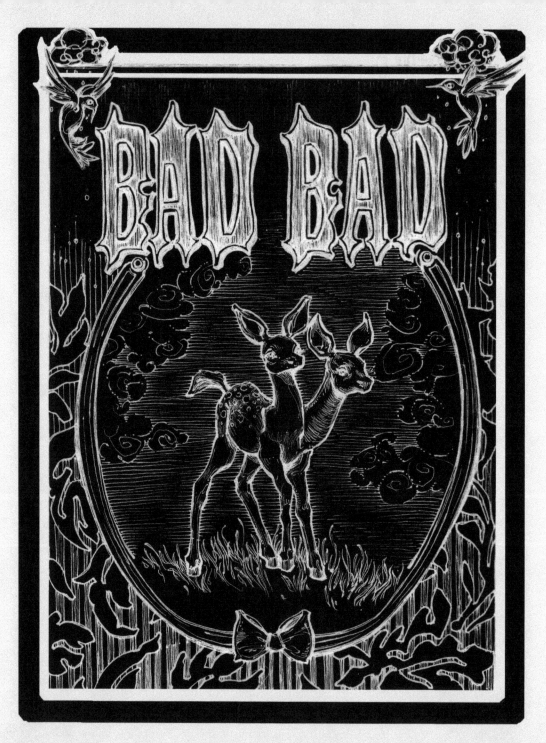

National Suicide Prevention Lifeline
1-800-273-8255

also by Chelsey Minnis

Poemland
Baby I Don't Care

Printed in the USA
CPSIA information can be obtained
at www.ICGtesting.com
JSHW051041070524
62693JS00007B/67